Food Justice: A Primer

Edited by

Saryta Rodríguez

Sanctuary Publishers

ISBN-13: 978-0-9989946-3-5

Sanctuary Publishers, www.sanctuarypublishers.com

-A Book Publisher That Gives Back-

Cover designer: Danae Silva Montiel
Content editor: Julia Feliz Brueck

DEDICATION

To my mother, Iris Margarita Rodríguez,
to whom all of my life's work is dedicated.
I am who I am because you showed me the way.

And to the indomitable spirit of the people of Puerto Rico,
who lead by example by coming together
in times of hardship,
sacrificing neither faith nor pride.
Tierra linda mía, yo te quiero.

CONTENTS

PREFACE

In 2016, nearly thirteen percent of U.S. Americans were living in poverty, a third of whom were children under the age of eighteen. Over forty-one million U.S. Americans lived in food-insecure homes, including nearly thirteen million children.[1] The World Food Summit of 1996 defined *food security* as "when all people, at all times, have physical and economic access to sufficient, safe and nutritious food that meets their dietary needs and food preferences for an active and healthy life."[2] In other words, while roughly 40,600,000 million U.S. Americans qualified as impoverished in 2016, an additional 600,000 still did not have consistent, reliable access to healthful food.

Figures from abroad often paint an even more dismal picture of food justice, or lack thereof, around the world. It's something everyone knows about, deep down; we all know that it's happening, day in and day out— people are starving, ailing and dying due to malnutrition, diabetes and other illnesses that are directly correlated with what we eat (or don't eat). While initiatives abound in response to the question, "Why are there so many hungry people in the world, and what can we do to fix it?" many of these initiatives support animal agriculture, which in fact directly hinders food justice on a number of levels. Food justice initiatives also commonly fail to recognize the unique struggles of marginalized members of our society to obtain healthful food for themselves and their families.

This is why I was— am— so compelled to present the enclosed compilation. Herein lies a collection of essays regarding food justice, *through a vegan praxis*, by which I mean that this book explores solutions to hunger and food insecurity that are void of animal agriculture. For too long, the vegan community and the food justice community have been unnecessarily at odds with one another, competing for resources, media attention, and playing Oppression Olympics, with advocates on each side asserting that their cause is more important than the other.[3]

In reality, these two causes are inextricably linked. While ending animal agriculture would certainly not immediately end world hunger, it would go a long, *long* way. Similarly, veganism would undoubtedly spread much more easily into various communities around the world if consistent access to fresh produce were prioritized. I'm not just talking about the "Third World," either; these problems persist right here in the U.S., including in some of the wealthiest states in the Union, such as New York and California.

Aside from the role of nonhuman animals in our society, food justice both influences and is influenced by a myriad of factors to such an extent that exploring the issue can be quite overwhelming. Environmental factors— which are influenced both by reliance on nonhuman animal agriculture and unsustainable crop-farming methods—play a key role, as well as disturbing legal trends that seek to criminalize potential solutions to hunger. Shockingly, there are legal initiatives taking place in parts of the U.S. seeking to actively *prevent* well-meaning individuals and organizations from giving away food! This form of altruism— whether taking the form of an individual handing another individual half of a sandwich or an organization preparing an entire meal for a crowd of homeless people—is thus not merely frowned upon (when it should be applauded) by the State, but, in some cities and towns, penalized via exorbitant fines and even arrest.

Food waste is yet another crucial and depressing factor. The truth is that there is enough food in the world, *right now*, to feed every hungry person on the planet. The issue of world hunger is not one of *supply*, but one of *distribution*, which is impacted both by multinationals that artificially inflate costs and by the simple fact that those who can regularly afford food in the U.S. habitually throw away leftovers, unwanted items and items that are approaching, but have not yet undergone, expiration. Grocery stores also throw away a shocking amount of food, though some have recently spearheaded initiatives to combat this through acts such as donating food to organizations that will distribute it and offering near-expiration foods at a significant discount so as to persuade consumers to purchase them.

There are some issues related to *food* and *justice* that are seldom addressed under the umbrella of "food justice." For instance, xenophobia and racism often result in unfair trade deals and other practices that put non-American farmers at a major disadvantage and perpetuate hunger abroad—particularly in Mexico— while disproportionately limiting access to healthful food among Americans of color.

It is my sincere hope that the works herein will help to build that all-important bridge between those who want to feed humans worldwide, those who want to protect nonhumans from captivity and violence, and those humans who actively produce the food of which we speak— farmers and farm laborers. I hope to hold the term *food justice* accountable on the *justice* end, ensuring that the solutions we explore together to answer the increasingly urgent problem of healthful food access enforce justice for humans and nonhumans alike. I also hope that this primer will serve as a strong foundation for those who are interested in this topic but are unfamiliar with some of its many facets. Though this volume is by no means the end-all and be-all of the issue, it might serve as a good place to start.

For your convenience, I have included an annotated mini-glossary just before the first chapter of this book. The glossary aims to disambiguate food justice lingo and parallel terms (by, for instance, offering distinctions between *food justice*, *food sovereignty* and *food security*), as well as to caution against overreliance on certain popular but fundamentally meaningless marketing terms, such as *cruelty-free* and *humane.*

I knew as soon as I conceptualized it that this project would be too big for me alone. I couldn't possibly do all of these topics justice (which is, after all, the Word of the Day), as while I have a wealth of experience in some areas, I have little or no experience in others. I would like to extend my utmost, sincere gratitude to the contributors whose works you will encounter herein, who have lent their experiences, insights and intuitions to this volume, and from whom I have learned so much.

Yours,

S. Rodríguez

Citations

1. "Poverty and Hunger Fact Sheet." *Feeding America*, September 2017.

2. "Food Security." *Policy Brief*, published by the Food and Agriculture Organization of the United Nations. Issue 2, June 2006.

3. Rodríguez, Saryta. "Oppression Olympics and the Pitfalls of 'Animal Whites.'" *Reasonable Vegan*, July 31, 2015.

INTRODUCTION

An Overview of the Food Justice Movement, 1960s-Present

By Saryta Rodríguez

So much has happened in the realm of food justice that choosing an era or timespan on which to focus presents a challenge. Even within such a timespan, individual actions and local, regional and national concerns are so vast and frequent that it would be impossible to cover them all in these introductory pages. That said, herein I will endeavor to describe some of the more global, pervasive issues that arise within the movement and what actions have been regularly taken to combat them.

For starters, I find it important to clarify why I have chosen to move ahead with this project under the banner of food justice rather than sovereignty or security, so allow me to briefly disambiguate these terms.

Food Justice: The belief that food is a basic right of all people.[1] The Food Justice Movement, by extension, is a struggle to preserve this right and ensure that *all* people have access to it, regardless of race, gender, religion, sexual orientation, socioeconomic status, or any other factor or feature of their lives.

Food Sovereignty: A population's right to determine *how* it is fed.[2] This is the source of many more nuanced discussions in the Food Justice Movement, beyond simply whether or not people have a right to be fed; for instance, many peasant-led campaigns around the world against GMOs (which will be discussed later in this Introduction) argue not against the scientific benefits or utility of GMOs— Genetically-Modified Organisms, specifically crop seeds— but against the legal and economic mechanisms through which multinational corporations often employ these *against the will of local food growers*, or even "pressure" (force) local food growers to employ these against their own will.

Food Insecurity: A household-level economic and social condition of limited or uncertain access to adequate food.[3] The pervasiveness of food insecurity around the world illustrates that the right to food is far from universal at the moment, and this is a problem the Food Justice Movement wishes to alleviate.

The Food Justice Movement involves both food sovereignty and food security as two primary concerns. An example of an effort to uphold food sovereignty can be found in Palestine, where, in 1986, The Union of Agricultural Work Committees (UAWC) was established. The UAWC sought to improve the difficult social and economic situation of Palestinian farmers that resulted from the marginalization of agriculture and confiscation of land and water resources under Israeli occupation. According to its Grassroots International page, the UAWC "emphasizes sustainable development and food sovereignty rather than emergency and relief projects. The UAWC also helps Palestinian farmers market their produce and provides agricultural employment and training opportunities through cooperation agreements with domestic, Arab and international agricultural development institutions. Local agricultural committees in the West Bank and Gaza Strip formed by the UAWC assess farmers' priorities and involve them in implementing self-help programs and community activities."[4]

Thus, even while the right to food may have been upheld by aid organizations and other volunteer efforts, the UAWC seeks for the people of Palestine to determine for themselves *how* they would be fed, and to develop systems that allow them to sustainably feed themselves without outside assistance or temporary solutions.

An example of an effort to combat food insecurity on a local level can be found in New York, where the Green Bronx Machine was founded. Based in the South Bronx—where half of all households receive SNAP (Supplemental Nutrition Assistance Program) benefits, a strong indication of food insecurity (to put that in perspective, only about 13% of households across the United States received such benefits in 2015);[5] and where "99% of students qualify for free and reduced lunch while the 99-cent menu stalks them at every corner"[6]— this organization teaches students how to grow and harvest vegetables at school for themselves and their families.

Other priorities within the Food Justice Movement include:

- *Workers' rights:* The ability of those working "in food," at all levels, to earn a living wage, experience safe working conditions, access education for their children, be protected from exploitative work hours, and so forth; and

- *Land rights:* These are extremely location-dependent and are dug into more deeply in the chapter "Case Study and Interview: Occupy the Farm," beginning on Page 123. While in some cases, *ownership* of the land is critical (as is often the case for the MST in Brazil, a group whose members rely on public lands not only to feed themselves but for their very survival), in others, the focal point is land *use* (such as the case with Occupy The Farm in Berkeley, California, in which the surrounding community relied heavily on land owned by UC Berkeley for food but did not need to live on this land or use it in any other way).

- *The role of technology in feeding humanity:* This concern is best illustrated by the ongoing debate regarding the use of GMOs (Genetically-Modified Organisms), summarized later in this Introduction.

- *The preservation of human rights:* While related to workers' rights more broadly, I feel that this point requires individual attention as it applies to different workers differently. While long hours, for instance, or low pay, are issues that painfully impact *all* farm workers, there are other risks involved for specific social demographics. For instance, children are often kidnapped and enslaved to work on chocolate farms on the Ivory Coast and elsewhere.[7] Women in the food industry— around the world and, in the U.S. specifically, many migrant women coming from Mexico to farm— are often sexually assaulted.[8]

Workers' Rights Campaigns

Perhaps the most famous names in farm workers' rights here in the U.S. are Cesar Chavez and Dolores Huerta. Together, they formed the National Farm Workers' Association (NFWA) in 1962. (This would later become known as United Farm Workers, or UFW, which is still active today.) Among the group's early priorities were to ensure that farm workers were fairly compensated for their labor and that state laws regarding agricultural working conditions were upheld.[9]

Throughout the 1960s, Chavez and the NFWA engaged in a series of activities toward these ends, including, but not limited to:

- The foundation and regular publication of *El Malcriado: The Voice of the Farm Worker,* beginning in 1964.
- The Delano Grape Strike.
- The Salad Bowl Strike.

The Delano Grape Strike began on September 8, 1965, and lasted more than five years. The strike centered on the demand that farm workers receive wages equal to the federal minimum wage, and included both a workers' strike against grape growers and a local grape boycott. In March of 1966, Chavez lead a 250-mile march from Delano to Sacramento, California, to let the public and lawmakers know about the mistreatment of farm workers. The NFWA encouraged all U.S. Americans to boycott table grapes as a show of support. This led to a nationwide boycott of California grapes in 1968.

A review outlining the strikes published on Seed the Commons notes that,[10]

> *The Delano Grape Strike ended in 1970. NFWA— now UFW— won the following, according to Rolling Stone:*
>
> *The UFW spent five years on strike and boycotting to win their original contracts with the table grape industry. Before the Union's victory, base wage in grapes was $1.20 an hour with a ten to 20¢ kickback to the labor contractor. The 1970 union agreement started at $2.05 and created the first hiring hall in grape-growing history. It also forced the growers to accept pesticide regulations much stiffer than the state of California's, an employer-financed health plan, banning workers under 16, and no firing without just cause.*[11]
>
> *In Salinas, CA, 6,000 driving and packing workers represented by the Teamsters, a rival union, took this opportunity to go on strike themselves, disrupting the lettuce supply. An agreement resulted from this weeklong strike in which the Teamsters— but not the NFWA— were given access to farms and the right to organize into unions. Growers in California began to sign "sweetheart contracts" with the Teamsters to avoid compliance with UFW terms. Under the threat of being fired, farm workers*

were pressured to consent to Teamsters contracts that "ignored the wishes of the workers, arranged only because the growers felt threatened by the economic and social revolution fomented by Cesar Chavez, the farm union president."[12] Chavez went on a hunger strike to protest this development, and, about a month later, two large companies broke ranks with the rest of the lettuce industry and signed contracts with NFWA.

These agreements ultimately collapsed, however, and within weeks the largest US farm worker strike in history took place: The Salad Bowl Strike. By September 1970, Chavez was calling on all U.S. Americans to boycott any lettuce that was not picked by NFWA workers. He was arrested in November, released in December, and immediately instigated a boycott once again, this time with six additional lettuce growers.[13]

Finally, in March 1971, The Teamsters and the NFWA signed an agreement which reaffirmed the latter's right to organize.

However, the fight did not end there. The early Seventies saw more protests, boycotts, arrests and violence surrounding this issue, as the Teamsters resumed their legal dispute with NFWA in December 1972 and the NFWA, in turn, threatened to call for a national boycott of any grower who signed a contract with the Teamsters in April 1973. These experiences ultimately provoked Chavez to advocate for legal reform, and led to the Modesto March of 1975, in which NFWA— now UFW— members marched from San Francisco to Modesto. The march, in turn, pressured Governor Jerry Brown to push for labor law reform, resulting in the passage of CALRA— The California Agricultural Labor Relations Act— in 1975.[14]

Despite this achievement, the review on Seed the

Commons examining the strikes further explains that,[15]

Unfortunately, many of the problems organizations like NFWA/UFW have been trying to address since the 1960s persist today. While in 1985, six years after UFW negotiated a deal with Sun World (a major citrus and grape grower) that brought farm worker wages up to $5.25 per hour at a time when minimum wage was only $2.90, many didn't even make the day's minimum wage in 2015[16]*— and they certainly did not make dollars more per hour beyond it:*

In 1979, the United Farm Workers negotiated a contract with Sun World, a large citrus and grape grower. The contract's bottom wage rate was $5.25 per hour. At the time, the minimum wage was $2.90. If the same ratio existed today, with a state minimum of $9.00, farm workers would be earning the equivalent of $16.30 per hour. At the end of the 70s, workers under union contracts in lettuce and wine grapes were earning even more.

Today farm workers don't make anywhere near $16.00 an hour.

In 2008, demographer Rick Mines conducted a survey of 120,000 migrant farm workers in California from indigenous communities in Mexico – Mixtecos, Triquis, Purepechas and others. "One third of the workers earned above the minimum wage, one third reported earning exactly the minimum and one third reported earning below the minimum," he found.

In other words, growers were potentially paying an illegal wage to tens of thousands of farm workers.[17]

Perhaps not surprisingly, many of the same methods employed to challenge these injustices in the 1960s and

1970s have survived to the present day. From a legal perspective, in September of 2016— fewer than *two years* ago, and over fifty years since NFWA/UFW was founded— Governor Jerry Brown was lauded by the *LA Times* and other outlets for expanding overtime pay for California farm workers. The bill was sponsored by UFW leaders, who called Brown's decision "a victory in a nearly 80-year quest to establish broad rights and protections for farm laborers."[18]

From the perspective of grassroots organizing, the Driscoll Strike, which lasted for roughly three years, also "ended" in September 2016— within a week or two of Gov. Brown's overtime expansion. Familias Unidas por la Justicia (Families United for Justice), a local farm worker union affiliated with the Washington State Labor Council, led this strike against Sakuma berry growers (whose berries are marketed and sold by Driscoll's and found in grocery stores across the U.S.).[19] Workers hoped to be granted permission to have a union in order to raise wages and improve working conditions; they often worked 12-hour days picking berries for merely $6 a day.[20]

While some outlets reported that the strike "ended" as Sakuma finally agreed to "allow a union election and recognize and bargain a contract with the union, Familias Unidas por la Justicia (FUJ), if it won,"[21] the truth— as was the case with the Salad Bowl strike— is more complex. Many are still engaged in this boycott, hoping that the union rights recently granted to U.S. American farm workers will be expanded to include their counterparts across the border.[22]

Land Rights Campaigns

Brazil's Landless Workers' Movement (MST)—one of the largest social movements in Latin America, with an estimated informal membership of 1.5 million people[23]— has "inspired many others to see land occupations as a hopeful tactic for achieving land access."[24] The Landless Workers' Movement was born through a process of occupying *latifundios* (large, landed estates) and officially became a national movement in 1984. The movement has led to over 2,500 land occupations and resulted in the reclamation of 7.5 million hectares of previously unproductive land for farming purposes. Families who now live and farm on this land continue to advocate for better education, credit for agricultural production and cooperatives, and access to health care through MST.[25]

The MST occupations have resulted not only in successful settlement of this land but also in the gaining of *legal titles* to the land[26]— though it is worth noting that the movement maintains it is already immediately entitled to occupy any unproductive land (with or without the granting of any titles), owing to a section in Brazil's most recent Constitution (1988) that states land should fulfill a social function.[27] MST also notes that, based on 1996 census statistics, 3% of the Brazilian population owns two-thirds of all "arable" (farmable) land in Brazil.[28]

Another example of a land rights campaign that seeks to give people lawful ownership of land is the South African Shack Dwellers movement, also known as Abahlali baseMjondolo or AbM. This movement was formed in 2005 to "fight for, promote and advance the interests and dignity of shack dwellers and other impoverished people."[29] At a conference in Oslo, Norway, Thapelo Mohapi spoke of the movement's relationship to land and attitudes toward land ownership:

Land is fundamental to our struggle. We have occupied and held land in many new land occupations. We have also successfully resisted many evictions from old land occupations through popular protest and by using the courts. We have kept thousands of families on their land and in their homes. But, most importantly, we have built a politically conscious movement where we can, thinking together, develop a better understanding of poverty and what keeps us in poverty. Through the movement we can build our power together and organize and struggle for justice together. We are committed to a society and a world in which land, wealth and power are shared on an equal basis.[30]

In both cases cited above, efforts are being made to reclaim land not only for agricultural purposes, but also for sheer *living* purposes— including housing. Vastly more common in the United States are movements aimed at reserving land specifically for agricultural and/or food distribution purposes, without the additional burdens of trying to secure legal ownership of land or rights to long-term occupancy. Two examples of this are Occupy the Farm and the work of the Bay Area Food Not Bombs, both of which are based in Berkeley, California. Occupy the Farm began in 2011 in response to UC Berkeley's attempt to sell and develop part of the Gill Tract, which the university had previously been using for agricultural research while allowing crops to be distributed to those in need. The university planned to use this land for biotech research instead— research which would no longer require that crops be grown at all.

This posed a significant risk to those who relied on Gill

Tract produce, and as a result, scores of people participated in occupying the land as well as "guerilla gardening"—planting and harvesting at risk of arrest while continuing to distribute food to those in need. Gustavo Oliviera, Occupy the Farm spokesperson, discusses the movement in his interview, beginning on Page 123.

Just a stone's throw away from the Gill Tract is People's Park, land also owned by UC Berkeley but claimed by Bay Area Food Not Bombs members back in the Sixties as a place for the homeless to sleep and to receive vegan meals prepared and served for free by the organization. Residents of People's Park habitually face eviction as the university routinely threatens to replace the park with an athletic field or more labs. In conjunction with these efforts to evict the homeless, efforts threatening the work of Food Not Bombs and other organizations are taking place nationwide, as "feeding bans" in various forms place restrictions on who can give food to whom, where, and when. Sadly, people have already been arrested for the simple act of handing food to a hungry person. We explore feeding bans and potential solutions under "Food Waste, Feeding Bans, and the Criminalization of Dissent," starting on Page 67.

Food Sovereignty and the Great GMO Debate

Today, the world has about 7.6 billion inhabitants.[31] Most demographers believe that by about 2050, that number will reach roughly 10 billion.[32] So, a big issue in the Food Justice Movement today is the question of how we can be prepared to feed that many people just over thirty years from now. Even with the understanding that current food shortages are often the result of inequitable distribution and waste, the amount of food currently being produced on the planet may be enough to feed 7 or even 8 billion humans, but is likely insufficient to feed 10 billion.

Enter GMOs. Larger crops[33] and higher yields[34] are examples of reasons given for researching and disseminating genetically-modified seed. On the other side of the coin, there are those who believe technology is insufficient for saving planet Earth, and that it is more essential for humans to change their behaviors in order to protect our planet and ensure that it stays healthy enough to produce the food we need. These people are focused not on developing scientific methods of producing more food than we currently do, but rather on drastically reducing our consumption and improving upon our environmental stewardship. Examples of this ideology in practice include:

- **Veganism.** While more often cited as a milder form of advice, such as "eat less meat" or "go vegetarian" rather than "go vegan," these all stem from the fact that meat consumption, aside from its myriad ethical implications, is unsustainable as our population rises. Pound for pound, meat has a much higher water footprint than vegetables, grains, and beans do. For instance, a single pound of beef takes, on average, 1,800 gallons of water to produce.[35]

For those who do profess some empathy for nonhumans (though not enough to consider their murder completely out-of-bounds), it is often noted that there is simply not enough land available on the planet Earth to allow for every farmed animal to be farmed according to "humane" standards, which imply outdoor space to roam and the ability to graze, among other things. The results of one of the largest examples of roaming "grass-fed" cattle can be seen in the degradation of the Amazon rainforest. According to a 2015 study, beef "production" was the leading driver behind deforestation, followed by soybean production (the majority used as livestock feed).[36] Cattle ranching accounts for 80 percent of deforestation rates within all regions of the Amazon. The main use of cleared land is cattle pasture.[37] According to the Yale School of Forestry and & Environmental Studies, "Cattle ranching in the Amazon region is a low yield activity, where densities often average just one cattle per hectare...In Brazil, pasture land outweighs planted cropland by about 5 times."[38] Adding to the problem, the Food and Agriculture Organization explains that, "overgrazing and nutrient loss turn the rainforest land that was once a storehouse of biological diversity into an eroded wasteland. [39]

- **Recycling, composting, and avoiding products like plastic.** Campaigns for eco-friendlier living abound today. More and more, everything from coffee cups to disposable forks to water bottles is being developed in more sustainable ways, such as using recyclable plastic and using compostable plant-based materials. Companies are responding to consumer concerns by creating these and using them at service businesses such as restaurants and cafes, while consumers themselves are being challenged to change their habits in small but significant ways, such as purchasing one reusable water bottle rather than constantly buying water on-the-go and bringing one's own reusable bags to the grocery store. Indeed, in some parts of the U.S., plastic grocery store bags have been outright banned.[40]

These positions are not mutually exclusive. It is, of course, possible to be optimistic about GMOs and still choose to go vegan. One can support maximizing crop yields technologically and also eschew non-recyclable plastic. The distinction lies with the preferred strategy, the overarching school of thought— which we'll delve into more deeply in just a minute.

Unfortunately, there are some persistent problems with the way GMOs are being implemented presently that are quickly turning food justice advocates against them. Chief among these is the employment of *patents* by multinational corporations, such as Monsanto. A patent is a set of exclusive rights granted by a sovereign state or intergovernmental organization to an inventor or assignee for a limited period of time in exchange for detailed public disclosure of an invention.[41] As GMO companies patent their seeds against *biopiracy*— or biological ripping-off by competitors— the patent applies to any seed that bears similar "genetic information" to the patented one. An unintended consequence of this is that many farmers and peasants who have been growing seeds for generations, in non-GMO ways, find their work threatened.

It is a common feature of GMO debates nowadays for people to label themselves and others as "pro-GMO" or "anti-GMO." In my view, these labels are too vague and, therefore, do more harm than good. It is often assumed, for instance, that someone who is "pro-GMO" supports the right of multinationals to patent a wide variety of seed properties, as is the current practice; or that someone who is "anti-GMO" doesn't understand the science behind genetic modification and is therefore irrationally skeptical of the process.

Enter Charles Mann. In his recent book, *The Wizard and the Prophet*, Mann brilliantly outlines the schools of thought from which debates like that over GMOs stem. Prophets can trace their ideology back to William Vogt, the unofficial "founder" of the modern environmental movement. Vogt exemplified "what the Hampshire College population researcher Betsy Hartmann has called 'apocalyptic environmentalism'— the belief that unless humankind drastically reduces consumption and limits population, it will ravage global ecosystems."[42] Wizards can trace their ideology back to Norman Bourlag, who has become "the emblem of 'techno-optimism'—the view that science and technology, properly applied, will let us produce a way out of our predicament."[43]

Again, these categories are not mutually exclusive, and it is at least possible if not preferable to make drastic lifestyle changes to protect the environment while also supporting cutting-edge research that can improve upon our ability to feed ourselves. Where Wizards and Prophets differ is not in terms of their end goal, but in the method they trust most. Unfortunately, Wizards often dismiss Prophets as Luddites, while Prophets accuse Wizards of deluding themselves by thinking they can come up with a quick fix to combat centuries-long environmental devastation.

In an article for *The Atlantic*, Mann writes:

Wizards view the Prophets' emphasis on cutting back as intellectually dishonest, indifferent to the poor, even racist (because most of the world's hungry are non-Caucasian). Following Vogt, they say, is a path toward regression, narrowness, poverty, and hunger—toward a world where billions live in misery despite the scientific knowledge that could free them. Prophets sneer that the Wizards' faith in human resourcefulness is unthinking, ignorant, even driven by greed (because refusing to push beyond ecological limits will cut into corporate profits). High-intensity, Borlaug-style industrial farming, Prophets say, may pay off in the short run, but in the long run will make the day of ecological reckoning hit harder. The ruination of soil and water by heedless overuse will lead to environmental collapse, which will in turn create worldwide social convulsion. Wizards reply: That's exactly the global humanitarian crisis we're preventing! As the finger-pointing has escalated, conversations about the environment have turned into dueling monologues, each side unwilling to engage with the other.[44]

As a Prophet, I can't resist advising against mistaking something that can *help* feed people for a "solution" to meeting all of their nutritional needs. For instance, there was, rightfully, a great deal of celebration when it was discovered that rice, the primary food for myriad populations around the world, can be genetically modified to include Vitamin A and other nutrients it does not traditionally contain. This new rice is commonly referred to as "golden rice."[45] While this will certainly go a long way in helping those who currently subsist exclusively off of rice get more nutrients, it is important that we not just disseminate this rice and call it a day. We must instead continue to investigate the question of *why these populations only have rice to eat in the first place.* Diversity in one's diet is essential, and no single crop, no matter how technologically enhanced, can currently meet *all* of any human's nutritional needs. So although this rice will help address a very serious condition for those affected, we still need to get to the bottom of this, and empower communities to access, grow and distribute crops other than rice.

Campaigns for the Preservation of Human Rights

What follows is a small sampling of the many, *many* human rights campaigns taking place within the realm of food justice.

Campaigns for Women

Women in the food industry face myriad forms of violence, including but not limited to rape. Campaigns have been organized by female agricultural workers focusing on violence against all women, while other activities focus on empowering women in the food industry specifically— not only protecting them from violence but also allowing them autonomy and means of economic growth equal to that experienced by men in their communities doing the same work.

To the former point, in December 2017, women in Brazil's MST movement, mentioned above (and further explored in "Case Study & Interview: Occupy the Farm," beginning on Page 123), occupied the farm of Dr. Roger Abdelmassih, condemned in 2010 to 278 years in prison for raping 39 women, most of whom were his patients. The women of MST released a public statement saying that they "continue to fight for the right to land and for agrarian reform policies; against machismo and violence against women and LGBTs; and against the culture of rape."[46]

In February 2011, Via Campesina launched a campaign in Africa condemning violence against women. This campaign included the following elements:

- Starting or taking part in national campaigns in

order to pass legislation guaranteeing women's rights and denying impunity to those who commit violence against women and children.

- Organizing public actions condemning violence and its causes, in order to prevent violence before it occurs.

- Reinforcing alliances and partnerships with national, regional and international organizations which fight violence against women and for the defense and respect of women's rights, particularly the World Women's March.

- Fight for parity in our organizations, guarantee women's participation in decision making and their visibility in public events, as well as encourage the creation of specific women's areas.[47]

With respect to empowering women in agriculture specifically, on March 8, 1996, Zapatista women celebrated International Women's Day by taking the city of San Cristóbal de las Casas, demonstrating in the streets with signs, slogans, songs, and dances. They asserted that they are not free simply by being Zapatista, as they are still subject to domination and oppression by Zapatista men.[48]

The First International Assembly of Women Farmers was held in Bangalore, India, on October 1, 2000. The Assembly adopted three major goals:

1. Ensure the participation of 50% of women at all levels of decisions and activities,

2. Maintain and strengthen the Women's Commission, and
3. Ensure that documents, training events and speeches of Via Campesina did not have sexist content or sexist language.[49]

The Second International Assembly of Women Farmers was held as part of a Via Campesina conference in Sao Paolo, Brazil, on June 1, 2004. This assembly brought together more than a hundred women from 47 countries on all continents. The main lines of action that emerged from the meeting were to take action against physical and sexual violence against women, both domestically and internationally; demand equal rights, and invest in education.[50]

On October 1, 2006, women from Asia, North America, Europe, Africa and Latin America met at the World Congress of Women in Santiago de Compostela, Spain, to discuss the meaning of equality in the field and a plan of action to achieve it. They faced three challenges:

1. Advance the theoretical discussion to incorporate the feminist peasant perspective in mainstream feminist analysis,
2. Continue work on autonomy as a vital reference for the consolidation of the movement of rural women, and
3. Overcome the feeling of guilt in the struggle for higher positions of power over men.[51]

Campaigns for Children

Unfortunately, children around the world are routinely abused by agricultural operations. Depending on where they are and who they "work" for, risks posed to children include kidnapping; regular beatings; forced, inhumane work hours in intense heat, with little or no monetary compensation; and strenuous physical demands, such as being expected to carry extremely heavy loads.

Food Empowerment Project, a U.S.-based organization working for the rights of farm workers and nonhuman rights, has done a lot to raise awareness of these issues within the chocolate industry specifically. The organization's website currently hosts a list of chocolate companies as well as information on whether or not they engage in these practices and whether a given company has ignored requests for this information or even outright refused to provide it. [52] This makes it easier for those who are just learning about these issues to avoid supporting companies that benefit from these practices with just the click of a button. (Food Empowerment Project also regularly helps support the needs of the children of farm laborers here in the U.S. by hosting events such as school supply drives.)

Here in the U.S., it has become more widely known in recent years that there is no legal age limit for children working on small farms with parental permission, and the conditions of this labor are far less regulated than other forms of labor. A documentary by Human Rights Watch entitled "Fingers to the Bone" interviewed child farm laborers in the U.S. and found that many of them suffered long hours, heat exposure and extreme physical demands, as well as, in some cases, limited access to education as they faced pressure from family to quit school in order to work more hours on the farm. The Children's Act for Responsible Employment, or CARE Act, has been regularly introduced to Congress since 2001, in an effort to address these issues and provide further protection to child farm laborers.[53] It was introduced in bill form in September 2009 by California Representative Lucille Roybal-Allard. Unfortunately, however, as of April 2018, it still has not been enacted.[54]

Campaigns for Immigrants in the U.S.

While undocumented immigrants in the United States have always faced some level of threat from Immigration and Customs Enforcement, or ICE, the Trump administration has made anti-immigration— legal and otherwise— a cornerstone of its agenda. Arrests of undocumented immigrants with no criminal records skyrocketed in 2017,[55] the first year of Trump's presidency, while both he and Sessions have condemned "sanctuary cities"— places in which local law enforcement is not obligated to cooperate with ICE agents in tracking down and deporting undocumented immigrants. In November 2017, a federal judge permanently blocked Trump's executive order to cut funding from sanctuary cities;[56] two months later, Attorney General Jeff Sessions threatened twenty-three sanctuary cities with subpoenas if they fail to provide documents to show whether local law enforcement officers are sharing information with federal immigration authorities.[57]

An unsurprising consequence of this is that undocumented immigrants across industries have become especially terrified of engaging in various aspects of life— such as going to work, reporting a crime or an accident, receiving medical care, or running errands— for fear that they or someone they love will be captured by an ICE agent. The fear of being arrested at work is particularly not unfounded; in January 2018, ICE agents targeted 7-Eleven stores in a series of nationwide immigration raids, sweeping a total ninety-eight stores.[58] Because so many agricultural workers in the U.S. are immigrants, and many of these are either undocumented or here on temporary work visas, the impact of this atmosphere is felt most palpably in the agricultural sector. According to researchers at the University of Southern California, undocumented people account for 45% of agricultural employment in California.[59]

These are people being targeted despite giving back to our society in one of the most fundamental ways: by feeding it.

Citations

1. "Food Justice." LexiconofFood.Com, accessed January 18, 2018.

2. Gayeton, Douglas. *LOCAL: The New Face of Food and Farming in America.* Harper Design, June 2014.

3. "Definition of Food Security." Published by the United States Department of Agriculture's Economic Research Service. Accessed January 15, 2018.

4. "Union of Agricultural Work Committees (UAWC)." *Grassroots International.* Accessed March 31, 2018.

5. "A Foodscape of the South Bronx." New York City Food Policy Center, Hunter College. Accessed March 31, 2018.

6. "About Us." GreenBronxMachine.Org. Accessed March 31, 2018.

7. "Child Labor and Slavery in the Chocolate Industry." *FoodisPower.Org*, accessed December 17, 2017.

8. "Sexual Assault and Farm Workers." NPR interview with Rosalinda Guillen. November 5, 2017.

9. Kim, Inga. "The Rise of the UFW." UFW.Org, April 3, 2017.

10. Rodríguez, Saryta. "Celebrating Cesar Chavez." SeedtheCommons.Org, April 21, 2016.

11. Harris, David. "The Battle of Coachella Valley: Cesar Chavez and UFW versus Teamsters." *Rolling Stone,* September 13, 1973.

12. Nordheimer, Jon. "Chavez and Teamsters Intensify Fight." *The New York Times,* September 8, 1975.

13. "Salad Bowl Strike." Wikipedia. Accessed March 31, 2018.

14. "Governor Signs Historic Farm Labor Legislation." *Los Angeles Times.* June 5, 1975.

15. Rodríguez, Saryta. "Celebrating Cesar Chavez." SeedtheCommons.Org, April 21, 2016.

16. Redmond, Tim. "Farm workers in California can barely survive in 2015."*48 Hills*, June 3, 2015.

17. Ibid.

18. Ulloa, Jazmine. John Myers. "In historic move, Gov. Jerry Brown expands overtime pay for California farm workers." *LA Times*, September 12, 2016.

19. "Washington farmworkers union ends boycott of Driscoll's, Sakuma." *NW Labor Press*, November 14, 2016.

20. Ahmad, Sameerah. "Strawberries and Solidarity: Farm Workers Build Unity around Driscoll's Berries Boycott." *TruthOut.Org*, March 1, 2017.

21. "Washington farmworkers union ends boycott of Driscoll's, Sakuma." *NW Labor Press*, November 14, 2016.

22. Ahmad, Sameerah. "Strawberries and Solidarity: Farm Workers Build Unity around Driscoll's Berries Boycott." *TruthOut.Org*, March 1, 2017.

23. "Landless Workers' Movement." Wikipedia entry. Accessed April 1, 2018.

24. Roman-Alcalá, Antonio. "Broadening the Land Question in Food Sovereignty to Northern Settings: A Case Study of Occupy the Farm." *Globalizations*, Vol. 12, Issue 4: Food Sovereignty: Concept, Practice, and Social Movements. Pages 545-558. 2015.

25. "What is the MST?" MSTBrazil.Org. Accessed February 4, 2018.

26. Roman-Alcalá, Antonio. "Broadening the Land Question in Food Sovereignty to Northern Settings: A Case Study of Occupy the Farm." *Globalizations*, Vol. 12, Issue 4: Food Sovereignty: Concept, Practice, and Social Movements. Pages 545-558. 2015.

27. "Landless Workers' Movement." Wikipedia entry. Accessed April 1, 2018.

28. Ibid.

29. Mohapi, Thapelo. "Popular Democratic Power is the Way to Challenge Inequality." Fighting Inequality: Talks on How to Change the World. Oslo, Norway. November 23, 2016.

30. Ibid.

31. World Population Clock. Accessed March 31, 2018.

32. "World population projected to reach 9.8 billion in 2050, and 11.2 billion in 2100." United Nations Department of Economic and Social Affairs. June 21, 2017.

33. Regalado, Antonio. "Super-Fast Growing GM Plants Could Yield the Next Green Revolution." *MIT Technology Review*, November 17, 2016.

34. Biello, David. "Norman Bourlag: Wheat breeder who averted famine with a 'Green Revolution.'" *Scientific American*, September 14, 2009.

35. "The Water Footprint of Food." Grace Communications Foundation. Accessed March 31, 2018.

36. Henders, Sabine. U Martin Persson. Thomas Kastner. "Trading forests: land-use change and carbon emissions embodied in production and exports of forest-risk commodities." *IOPScience.org*, December 22, 2015.

37. Nepstad, Daniel. "Slowing Amazon deforestation through public policy and interventions in beef and soy supply chains." *Science* magazine, October 2014.

38. "Cattle Ranching in the Amazon Region." Yale School of Forestry and Environmental Studies. Accessed June 6, 2018.

39. "Cattle Ranching and Deforestation." *Livestock Policy Brief 3*. Food and Agriculture Organization. Accessed June 6, 2018.

40. Editorial Board. "It's been a year since California banned single-use plastic bags. The world didn't end." *LA Times,* November 18, 2017.

41. "Patent." Wikipedia entry. Accessed April 1, 2018.

42. Mann, Charles. "Can Planet Earth Feed 10 Billion People?" *The Atlantic,* March 2018.

43. Ibid.

44. Ibid.

45. GoldenRice.Org. Accessed April 1, 2018.

46. "Women from Brazil's MST Occupy Farm Owned by Condemned Rapist." *Via Campesina*, December 5, 2017.

47. "Launch in Africa of the Via Campesina Campaign condemning violence against women." *Via Campesina,* February 21, 2011.

48. Muñoz-Ramírez, Gloria. *The Fire and the Word: a History of the Zapatista Movement.* Translated by Laura Carlsen with Alejandro Reyes Arias. San Francisco, California: City Lights Press, 2008.

49. Vivas, Esther. "La Via Campesina: Food Sovereignty and the Global Feminist Struggle." *Food First*, December 18, 2012.

50. Ibid.

51. Ibid.

52. F.E.P.'s Chocolate List. *Food Empowerment Project.* Accessed April 1, 2018.

53. "Long-awaited protection for child ag workers offered by CARE Act." *National Consumer's League*, June 2013.

54. "Children's Act for Responsible Employment." Wikipedia entry. Accessed April 1, 2018.

55. Hart, Benjamin. "Arrests of Undocumented Immigrants without Criminal Records Skyrocketed in 2017." *NY Magazine Daily Intelligencer*, February 12, 2018.

56. "Judge permanently blocks Trump sanctuary cities order." *NBC News*, November 21, 2017.

57. Johnson, Kevin. Gregory Korte. "DOJ threatens 'sanctuary cities' with subpoenas, escalating Trump's immigration enforcement campaign." *USA Today*, January 24, 2018.

58. Doubek, James. "ICE Targets 7-Eleven Stores in Nationwide Immigration Raids." *NPR*, January 11, 2018.

59. Khouri, Andrew. Geoffrey Mohan. "Visits by federal immigration authorities are spooking California businesses and workers." *LA Times*, February 26, 2018.

Making Connections "In the Name of Food"

By Julia Feliz Brueck

Cesar Chavez, farm worker rights activist and co-founder of the United Farm Workers union, once said,

> *...We cannot hope to have peace until we respect everyone—respect ourselves and respect animals and all living things. We know we cannot defend and be kind to animals until we stop exploiting them – exploiting them in the name of science, exploiting animals in the name of sport, exploiting animals in the name of fashion, and yes, exploiting animals* ***in the name of food.***

While the passages in this book attempt to make connections between food justice and prevalent issues that are often left out of discussions surrounding the movement, it is important to understand how nonhuman animal exploitation relates to social justice movements, including food justice. We can commence to make connections by understanding speciesism in terms of the interconnections between human and nonhuman oppression.

Systemic Supremacy

As an official term, veganism was coined in the 1940s as a way to verbalize the distinction between dietary vegetarianism and a way of living that rejected the use of nonhuman animals in all aspects, as practicable and possible, within a world that heavily relied (and still does) on their exploitation. This ethics-based concept, which extended beyond food choices, became known as veganism. This meant that those that chose veganism rejected the commodification, exploitation, and needless slaughter of other animals when alternatives were readily available.

In time, the oppressor-oppressed relationship between nonhumans and humans became cemented under a concept known as "speciesism." Simply put, the term encompasses the supremacist belief that humans are above nonhuman animals. This oppressive belief has allowed humans to "dominate" nonhumans and has resulted in the exploitative relationship that we hold with other animal species used for entertainment (zoos, aquariums, races, and circuses, just to name a few venues), testing (such as for the development of toiletries and cosmetics), clothing (wool, fur, leather), and, of course, food (animal agriculture, fisheries, etc). These are all practices that promote torture through mutilation, confinement, a denial of self, and eventual, slaughter – all without consent.

While the oppression between humans is not the same as nonhumans, both are rooted in systemic supremacy. Most recently, Donald Trump said of immigrants: "These aren't people. These are animals." Nonhumans have been traditionally "otherized," meaning they have been denigrated, denied personhood, and marginalized due to their obvious differences to humans, in order to justify them as "less than." In turn, nonhumans have been used to marginalize and justify the oppression of Black and Brown humans, forced to live in a system that protects whiteness as the "top" and "right" way to be. In this system, Black and Brown humans subconsciously learned and accepted to uphold their own otherization by also viewing and treating nonhumans as "less than" under what can be described as racialized speciesism (in my view, an aspect of speciesism experienced by people of color). This has culminated in a supremacist hierarchical relationship between all animals, human and nonhuman alike, which continues to ensure the survival of the oppressor/oppressed relationship that permeates myriad aspects of social justice, including food justice.

How has this worked? Animalization, even though we are all biological animals, is a tactic often employed to otherize marginalized groups. Donald Trump's latest comments on immigrants is an example of this, and we can see more examples of this tactic and how we reinforce it in the way we communicate daily. Consider something as basic as language and how terms that are even used today work to denigrate people of color, the disabled, and the poor, to name a few. How many commonly used words and phrases that we currently use originate from descriptions associated with nonhumans in a derogatory light (i.e. beast, pig, bitch, vulture, rat, savage, etc…)? How do those words continue to uphold the divide between humans (biologically animals) and nonhuman animals, the latter of whom are not even recognized as individual communities with their own languages, habitats, means of survival, and so forth? Subconsciously, we have played into our own version of supremacy and unwillingly and unquestioningly uphold it through the way we speak. Simply put, the language that we use reinforces the "less than" perception that humans have accepted of nonhumans without question. The same language is then continually employed to justify the perception that humans that do not fit a certain type are also "less than."

Interconnections to Food Justice

A shared oppression rooted in supremacy means that

speciesism and racism, for example, are intrinsically connected, and because of this, we cannot abolish one without the other. While veganism will not solve all the world's problems, understanding speciesism and how partaking in it also keeps people of color and other human groups oppressed is imperative:

It's important to keep in mind that the majority of people working in agriculture are people of color, including African American and Latinx. Many are migrant workers from Mexico and South America and undocumented. Other workers are refugees.

- **Factory Farm Workers**

Unsafe working conditions within factory farms include illness, injury, and even death from stress, accidents, as well as respiratory hazards, such as ammonia and other airborne particles that cross into the lungs through repeated exposure within factory farm operations. Unfortunately, due to isolation, language barriers, and the fear of losing their only source of income, most factory farm workers continue working under perilous conditions even when sick.[1]

- **Slaughterhouse Workers**

Slaughterhouse workers are also routinely exposed to hazardous working conditions and injuries due to reckless line speeds, long-working hours, and stress from repetitive movements involved in the slaughter and dismembering of hundreds of nonhumans each hour. The fast work pace means that many workers develop chronic physical ailments known as musculoskeletal disorders that cause strains and inflammation.[2] The Government Accountability Office (GAO) found that workers are often encouraged to continue working without seeking medical attention. Once again, many workers do not report their injuries or health conditions due to language barriers or fear of losing the job they depend on. Deaths, illness, and accidents, including amputations, are notoriously underreported according to GAO reports.[3]

- **Psychological Distress**

The repetitive violence witnessed and inflicted on nonhuman animals by workers are known to cause psychological disorders in slaughter house workers, including a post-traumatic stress disorder called perpetration-induced traumatic stress. A study on the effects within these conditions further concluded that "slaughterhouse employment increases total arrest rates, arrests for violent crimes, arrests for rape, and arrests for other sex offenses in comparison with other industries. This suggests the existence of a "Sinclair effect" [the negative effects of slaughterhouses on individuals and their communities] unique to the violent workplace of the slaughterhouse…"[4]

- **Environmental Racism**

The disproportionate negative impacts of pollution on people of color is commonly referred

> to as environmental racism or injustice.[5] The Food Empowerment Project explains that factory farms and slaughterhouses are, "considered a major contributor of pollution that affects the health of communities of color and low-income communities" due to their typical localization within these communities.[6] Intensive pig farms, for example, produce copious amounts of waste that are collected in cesspools and then sprayed on fields. This means that airborne toxins and noxious odors contribute to detrimental health conditions within these communities while leaks from cesspools and sprayed manure pollute ground and surface water.[7]

The above are examples of the interconnections between racism, food justice, and nonhuman exploitation. True, veganism is neither cruelty-free nor perfect; however, to reject nonhuman animal exploitation and thus, human supremacy, is to begin to also chip away at the oppression of marginalized people.

While issues abound in plant-based food agriculture, embracing a lifestyle change that rejects the system of oppression that is largely kept alive by what is on our plates, would be to take an even further stance against the destruction of our planet, against colonialism, against starvation, and against worker rights abuses rampant in the animal ag industry, which as discussed, depend largely upon vulnerable low-income communities of color. If we continue the conversation, we find that animal agriculture is further responsible for the displacement of Indigenous people and the destruction of wild areas, such as the Amazon, largely used as grazing areas for livestock or to grow crops as feed for the billions of nonhumans that will become served to people in other parts of the world. This is done while others starve despite there being sufficient amounts of food to feed populations of humans beyond the +7 billion that exist right now. The United Nations, as far back as 2010, publicly declared that a switch to plant-based diets would be intrinsic in fighting the effects of climate change, poverty, and starvation across the globe.[8]

When we examine the connections between human and nonhuman oppression and their detrimental impacts on both communities, can we truly justify our participation in speciesism when plant-based alternatives exist? Civil rights leader Angela Davis explained that, *I think there is a connection between...the way we treat animals and the way we treat people who are at the bottom of the hierarchy.* In a call to action, Davis said, *...it's the right moment to talk about it because it is part of a revolutionary perspective – how can we not only discover more compassionate relations with human beings but how can we develop compassionate relations with the other creatures with whom we share this planet and that would mean challenging the whole capitalist industrial form of food production.*

Consistent Anti-Oppression

In *The Dreaded Comparison*, Marjorie Spiegel boldly proclaimed the undeniable truth that *just as humans are oppressed the world over, [nonhuman] animals receive poor treatment in nearly every human culture on earth.* Spiegel added that we must reject the idea that one group is more important than another and we must be aware that this hierarchical acceptance in which we continuously place someone beneath us means that oppression will not end. Therefore, we must no longer view the liberation of humans and nonhumans as separate.

Consistent anti-oppression across all social justice groups, which includes an anti-speciesism stance, where *all* oppressor-oppressed relationships are disrupted and abolished should be the end goal. It is no longer enough to work towards justice without the awareness of root issues, without understanding the interconnections across oppressed species, and without rejecting supremacy between marginalized groups. As discussed in the introduction, the Food Justice Movement has been instrumental in working towards worker's rights, human rights (women, children, and immigrants), and even land rights.

In the words of Cesar Chavez, whom recognized the importance of consistent anti-oppression during his own work towards food justice, is it not time that we also include work against nonhuman exploitation done *"in the name of food?"*

Citations

1. "Factory Farm Workers." *Food Empowerment Project.* Accessed May 16, 2018.

2. "Working the Chain: Slaughterhouse Workers Face Lifelong Injuries." National Public Radio. Accessed May 17, 2018.

3. "Workplace Safety and Health: Additional Data Needed to Address Continued Hazards in the Meat and Poultry Industry." U.S. Government Accountability Office. Accessed May 16, 2018. https://www.gao.gov/products/GAO-16-337

4. Fitzgerald, A., Kalof, L., and Dietz, T. "An Empirical Analysis of the Spillover From "The Jungle" Into the Surrounding Community." *Sage Journal.* Volume: 22 issue: 2, page: 158-184. 2009.

5. Wing, S., Cole, D., and Grant, G. "Environmental Injustice in North Carolina's Hog Industry." *Environmental Health Perspectives.* Volume: 108 issue: 3, pages: 225-231. 2000.

6. "Environmental Racism." *Food Empowerment Project.* Accessed May 17, 2018.

7. Wing, S., Cole, D., and Grant, G. "Environmental Injustice in North Carolina's Hog Industry." *Environmental Health Perspectives.* Volume: 108 issue: 3, pages: 225-231. 2000.

8. "UN Urges Global Move to Meat and Dairy-free

Diet." *The Guardian*. Accessed May 17, 2018.

Further Reading

Veganism of Color, www.veganismofcolor.com

Food Empowerment Project, www.foodispower.org

Veganism in an Oppressive World: A Vegans-of-Color Community Project edited by Julia Feliz Brueck

Sistah Vegan: Black Female Vegans Speak on Food, Identity, Health, and Society by A. Breeze Harper

Aphro-ism: Essays on Pop Culture, Feminism, and Black Veganism from Two Sisters by Aph Ko and Syl Ko

The Jargon Section: Definitions & Discussions

Compiled and annotated
by Saryta Rodríguez

Enclosed in this section are both direct definitions for common food justice terms that are easily defined and longer discussions for more nuanced, less-strictly-defined terms. Many of these terms can be found in chapters throughout this book; where appropriate, notes are given about where you can look to find more information about a particular term. While some of these terms may not appear in multiple chapters, or even in any of them, they are nevertheless of great value to any reader who would like to continue investigating food justice issues beyond this primer.

Definitions: Community Supported Agriculture (CSA), Compost, Food Insecurity, Food Literacy, Permaculture, Seed Banks and Seed Swaps, and Veganic

Discussions: Biodiversity, Cruelty-Free, Dietary Colonization, Fair Trade, Fair Wild, Food Desert vs. Food Swamp, Food Justice vs. Food Sovereignty, Humane, and Sustainable.

Definitions

Community Supported Agriculture (CSA): "At the start of each growing season, members purchase a subscription. Each week they get a box of fresh produce containing whatever happens to be growing on the farm. That influx of cash at the start of the season allows the grower to purchase seed and farming implements, even hire workers. Essentially, a CSA subscription is a contract between a consumer and a farmer."[1]

Compost: "Turning food waste into valuable nutrients that can improve soil and feed plants."[2] For tips on how to get started, visit HowToCompost.org and/or Compost-Info-Guide.com.

Food Insecurity: A household-level economic and social condition of limited or uncertain access to adequate food. By contrast, the more commonly used term, "hunger," is an individual-level physiological condition that may result from food insecurity.[3]

Food Literacy: The ability of consumers to learn about agricultural practices, food production and food distribution such that they are able to discern which systems to support and which to shun.[4]

Permaculture: Wikipedia defines permaculture as "a system of agricultural and social design principles centered on simulating or directly utilizing the patterns and features observed in natural ecosystems." At the center of these principles are three ethics: earth care, people care and fair share.[5]

Earth Care: Rebuild natural capital. Recognize the Earth as a living entity, and nurture it.

People Care: Look after self, kin and community. Within a vegan framework, our definition of "community" broadens to include nonhuman animals as well as humans.

***Fair Share*:** Set limits and redistribute surplus.

This last principle is fundamental for vegans especially to grasp, as many vegans naively claim that, "If everyone went vegan, no one would go hungry." Without fair distribution of resources, the amount of resources in existence becomes irrelevant. Truth be told, there's already enough food on the planet for everyone to be fed *right now*.

These three ethics give rise to twelve design principles[6]:

1. Observe and interact.
2. Catch and store energy.
3. Obtain a yield.
4. Apply self-regulation and accept feedback.
5. Use and value renewable resources and services.
6. Produce no waste.
7. Design from patterns to details.
8. Integrate rather than segregate.
9. Use small and slow solutions.
10. Use and value diversity.
11. Use edges and value the marginal.
12. Creatively use and respond to change.

Seed Banks and Seed Swaps: Seed banks store seeds for the sake of preserving genetic diversity. They serve the practical function of allowing folks access to plants they need to increase crop yield, drought resistance, disease tolerance and other aspects of their crops; the environmental function of protecting biodiversity by storing seeds of plants that are endangered or inherently rare; and the cultural function of preserving plants that were used centuries ago, but not so much anymore, for their historical value.[7]

Seed swaps are events at which gardeners and farmers meet up to exchange seeds. This is a great way to cut down on your costs when starting your own garden or farm, while networking with others who may have more experience than you do and from whom you can glean valuable advice. They're also just downright fun!

Veganic: A farming method that does not use genetically modified seed, synthetic pesticides or synthetic fertilizers, and that does not use nonhuman animals in any way. Many organic-produce-farming operations rely on nonhuman waste as fertilizer, much of which comes from nonhuman-animal-exploitative farms. Therefore, these cannot be said to be fully "vegan," even if the farm on which these crops are grown does not exploit nonhuman animal directly. See Helen Atthowe's "Veganic Farming" for more information (beginning on Page 193).

Discussions

Biodiversity: the variety of life.[8] At the highest level, you can look at all the different species on the entire Earth. On a much smaller scale, you can study biodiversity within a pond ecosystem or a neighborhood park. While most people look at biodiversity through the lens of species diversity, two other important factors to consider are genetic biodiversity— the variation in genes that exists within a species— and ecological biodiversity: the diversity of ecosystems, natural communities and habitats. The latter addresses the myriad ways in which species interact with each other and their environment.

Biodiversity is essential to maintaining an abundance and variety of foods; stimulating economies; providing ecological services (such as cleaning our water and absorbing chemicals, as wetlands do, and providing oxygen for animals like us to breathe, as all plants do); and preventing disease, as is one primary function of genetic diversity.

Threats to biodiversity include climate change; habitat destruction; exploitative practices such as fishing, which is endangering ocean life, and land-animal farming, which leads to destruction of habitat for wild animals in addition to the murder of farmed animals themselves; and the spread of non-native species (such as when a genetically modified crop grown in one area is transported via pollinators to another crop and invades it)— all of which are linked to human activity. Reclaiming our food systems, minimizing and ultimately eliminating our reliance on large corporate food structures, and eschewing nonhuman animal agriculture are all important, positive steps we can take to protect what remains of our planet's biodiversity.

Cruelty-Free: A nonsense marketing term. Most products that are labeled "cruelty-free" are labeled such because they a) abstain from using nonhuman animal byproducts, b) abstain from testing products on nonhuman animals, or c) both a and b. However, neither the absence of nonhuman animal byproducts in an item nor the absence of testing on nonhumans prior to release of that item for sale ensures that it is truly free of cruelty.

Consider, for instance, a chocolate bar that is plant-based (i.e. does not contain milk, butter, cream or any other substance derived from nonhuman animals) and was, naturally, not tested on nonhumans before release, as I don't believe any chocolate bar ever is. Depending on how that chocolate was sourced, it may well have been grown using abhorrent labor practices, such as kidnapping young children and forcing them to work for hours on end, day in and day out, carrying sacks of exceptional weight on their backs and being beaten for not working quickly enough, or collapsing under said weight.[9] Such a chocolate bar cannot in good conscience be called "cruelty-free," independent of the ingredients therein besides the cocoa.

I personally would argue, though some self-identified vegans may disagree, that such a chocolate bar similarly cannot be called vegan, in spite of their plant-based content, as a primary tenet of veganism is to cause the least possible amount of harm, and chocolate can be harvested in ways that cause far less harm than that described above. Food Empowerment Project, a nonprofit organization dedicated to the protection of humans and nonhumans alike in food production and distribution, continuously compiles a list of chocolate purveyors that do not engage in abusive practices. This is list available both on Food Empowerment Project's website (www.foodispower.org) and as a downloadable iPhone app.

Dietary Colonization: This refers to the fact that as colonial powers such as England, Spain and the United States solidified their influence over less-developed countries, these powers introduced certain staple foods and food systems to the regions they colonized— often for worse instead of better— and, in many cases, continue to do so. For instance, the Columbian Exchange was a widespread transfer of animals, plants, culture, human populations, technology and ideas between the American and Afro-Eurasian hemispheres in the fifteenth and sixteenth centuries, following Columbus's arrival in America in 1492.[10] While Europe got mostly plants from America, such as maize (corn), potatoes, and tomatoes, America in return received goats, horses, chickens, cows and other nonhuman animals.

This not only led to a boom of animal agriculture in the US among white settlers, but the introduction of horses to America also resulted in many Native American tribes shifting from an (often plant-based) agricultural society to a nomadic society reliant on hunting. Not only did these changes result in myriad injustices against nonhuman animals, as they were exploited as both food and transportation, but it also wreaked havoc on Caribbean natives— human and nonhuman alike. Native nonhuman populations in the Caribbean suffered, while conucos, plots of land managed by indigenous peoples for sustenance, were damaged.

A more recent and ongoing example lies in the shift away from traditional food systems in Mexico, such as masa-based tortilla production (which Mexican consumers overwhelmingly purport tastes oh-so-much better)[11] to mass-produced corn tortillas made with flour, which comes with several negative consequences. First, it is a threat to the cultural heritage of Mexicans, as harvesting and crafting homemade tortillas was a cherished family tradition. Secondly, in the late 1980s small-scale tortillerias were incentivized to switch to the new flour-based method and punished for refusing to do so; in the words of Anthony DePalma of the New York Times, "...by the government, which sent them the worst corn and strictly limited the amount of grain the shops received. Hundreds of shops [went] out of business."[12] In this instance, we see that the very government of the colonized is to an extent cooperating with the colonizer for its own fiscal gain— at the expense of its own people.

Last but not least, the influx of cheap corn from the US to Mexico following the abolition of all tariffs on US corn sold in Mexico in 2007 put many Mexican corn farmers out of work.[13] The Mexican government has also withdrawn its price ceiling on corn tortillas, allowing corporations like Maseca-Gruma to make huge profit margins from selling corn tortillas in Mexico while Mexican corn farmers can barely make ends meet.

There is now a fast-growing movement to decolonize our diets for the sake of our health, in order to improve upon food sovereignty in many places, and in an effort to maintain our connection to our ancestral roots and to our planet.

Fair Trade: A certification for which companies must meet strict social, economic and environmental standards.

One such standard is that funds must be specifically designated for social, economic and environmental development projects, and the communities producing a particular product may choose for themselves what project would best fulfill their needs. For instance, Fair Trade "helps provide farming families with the income and stability they need to keep their children in school, instead of in the fields. From Nicaragua to India, farmer and worker associations have used Fair Trade funds to provide school supplies, pay for tuition and uniforms, set up scholarship programs, and finance free, healthy meals for children."[14]

Among other standards are: that farm workers and their families have access to doctors, medicine, vaccinations and health education; that sexual harassment not be tolerated and that all workers are provided with training to know their rights; and that farmers follow internationally monitored environmental standards, "while [Fair Trade is] empowering farmers and farm workers with financial incentives and resources for organic conversion, reforestation, water conservation and environmental education."

Fair Wild: A principle of maintaining sustainable, fair management and trading systems for wild-collected natural ingredients and products thereof.[15]

Foraging wild plants became increasingly mainstream in the early twenty-teens, with articles and videos by the likes of the New York Times's Mark Bittman providing useful guides for the uninitiated.[16] As with any new culinary trend, it is important that we go about our foraging in a way that neither disrupts local ecosystems nor disadvantages local wildlife. As companies emerge around these trends and develop products around these exciting new ingredients, we must also consider their labor practices, including hours per day a laborer works, that laborer's compensation and the treatment and conditions to which they are subjected.

Food Desert vs. Food Swamp: You've probably already heard the term food desert. This term has long been used to describe places where healthy, affordable, nutritious food is scarce, not for climate-related reasons such as in actual deserts or tundra, but for socioeconomic reasons. Low-income neighborhoods and neighborhoods of color in the US suffer disproportionately from this phenomena— and that's no accident.[17] There might be, say, twelve or thirteen listings for "grocery store" in such a neighborhood on the Internet, but if one takes the time to visit a handful of those listings it quickly becomes apparent that these are not all "grocery stores" in the sense that we initially imagine. Many are simply bodegas or corner-stores serving chips, beer, and, if you're lucky, some rotting bananas or apples tossed halfheartedly into a basket, assailed by flies. One cannot get the full amount of fresh produce one needs even to feed oneself, much less a family of four or five, from such a place.

More recently, folks in the food justice community have been switching over to employing the term food swamp instead, as this more accurately depicts the problem. The issue is not that there is a complete absence of food in these neighborhoods, as the image conjured by "food desert" implies, but rather that the food on offer is of neither sufficient quality nor sufficient diversity to meet the nutritional needs of humans.

The solution to food swamps is not, and cannot be, to stick a Whole Foods in every black-and-brown community in the US. This ignores the accessibility factor. Who cares if there are fresh greens, fruits and veggies just a few blocks away if you can't afford to buy them and there's a McDonald's just a block in the other direction, complete with a Dollar Menu to accommodate even the tightest of budgets? Thus, the conversation around food swamps (formerly known as food deserts) is twofold:

• How do we get existing businesses in these areas to increase their healthy food supply, and;

• How do we keep prices low when introducing new

food purveyors to an area so that everyone in the community can benefit from their presence, not just an influx of young techies or recent college graduates with trust funds?

This tightrope walk is especially pertinent with respect to community gardening. On one hand, this practice increases produce accessibility in a region; but, on the other hand, it also makes communities more attractive to higher-income folks and therefore has a tendency to speed up the process of gentrification— resulting in many of the folks who initially sowed, tended, and harvested the garden being displaced away from it, in the same manner that artists who beautify a previously neglected area are often driven out of it as the artwork they have created raises surrounding property values.

For more on the distinction between deserts and swamps and how each is calculated, see Starr Carrington's essay, "Food Justice and Race in the U.S.," beginning on Page 175.

Food Justice vs. Food Sovereignty: While similar in terms of both affected populations and strategies for solution, there is a slight difference between these two terms. Food justice refers to the belief that food is a basic right for all people,[18] while food sovereignty specifically refers to a population's right to decide how it is fed. The latter was coined in 1993 by a gathering of farm workers and small-scale food producers who later became the founders of La Via Campesina ("The Peasant's Way"), an organization that "...protects the rights of cultures to defend their control over local and regional food systems."[19]

This book employs food justice in its title so as to

reinforce the fact that all persons— regardless of race, gender or any other categorization— deserve food. The essays herein describe, among other things, the unique and specific challenges to food justice faced by various communities, including persons considered "of color" in the US, mothers, immigrants, farmers, and nonhumans. Some essays herein, such as Helen Atthowe's "Veganic Farming" (beginning on Page 193) and Dawn Moncrief's "Natural Resource and Food Sovereignty Benefits of Plant-Based Diets" (beginning on Page 107), may be useful in terms of strengthening the food sovereignty of the reader, their family and/or their local community.

Humane: Another nonsense marketing term— at least when applied to food production. The reality is that even foods that appear, on the surface, to be completely humane, such as strawberries and our aforementioned plant-based chocolate bar, are often not. Today, "humane" is used most predominantly to refer to nonhuman animal agricultural practices. To raise an egg-laying hen in a shed rather than a cage, for instance, is often called "humane." To allow cows to live and graze outside rather than in factory farm buildings is similarly called "humane" by food purveyors.

CertifiedHumane.Org defines "Certified Humane" on its FAQ page as follows:

The Certified Humane® Raised and Handled® label on meat, chicken, pork, eggs, pet food or dairy products means that the food comes from farms where Humane Farm Animal Care's precise, objective standards for the humane treatment of farm animals are implemented.[20]

No mention of what these "precise, objective standards" actually are appears on the page; however, if one scrolls down just a bit, a prime example of the label's disingenuousness emerges:

What's the difference between "debeak" and "beak trimming"– and what are Certified Humane's standards here?

No chicken is ever "debeaked" in our program, but our standards do call for "beak trimming" of the very tip of the beak. Here's why. One of the natural behaviors of chickens is pecking at each other to establish a dominance order – much like dogs in the pack fighting to establish the alpha, beta, and so on. The term, "pecking order" comes from centuries old observations of chickens, including the father of the domesticated chicken, the wild Red Jungle Fowl. When laying hens peck at each other, it's called "feather pecking."

Simply put, more aggressive birds attack less aggressive birds. It does not matter if the hens are indoors, outdoors or both. This is a natural behavior. In Sweden, where beak trimming was banned, they did a study comparing different housing systems. One of the things they discovered was regardless of the housing system, the highest cause of mortality (death) in laying hens was "cannibalism," which is perpetuated by pecking. Hens literally can peck each other to death. Regardless of flock size, all birds feather peck. We do not believe that high mortality due to cannibalism is humane. We believe the momentary discomfort of trimming a bird's beak when the bird is less than 10 days old is far more humane then allowing birds to cannibalize each other.[21]

The above passage presents us with both an instance of the all-too-common practice of sugarcoating a term to make it more palatable to consumers (the term "beak trimming" replacing "debeaking" and being presented as the more "humane" version of hen mutilation) and an example of the equally pervasive strategy of pitching violence against nonhumans as a necessity for their own good. We are asked to believe that hens who are not mutilated in one way or another will inevitably kill one another.

How is it possible, then, that, at myriad nonhuman animal sanctuaries across the planet, hens actually thrive? It is true that, regrettably, many rescued hens have already been debeaked or "beak-trimmed" prior to their arrival; but this is not the case for all of them. One also wonders how these animals could have survived in their own communities before humans intervened to "save" them by cutting off a part of their bodies. Finally, what CertifiedHumane.Org doesn't tell consumers is that hens who have had their beaks mutilated struggle to eat thereafter. I have witnessed this firsthand: a hen trying to scoop a worm off of the ground only to find it repeatedly falling out of her beak and back onto the ground; another hen experiencing a similar plight while trying to nab a bit of grain.

Human lips can be used to aid one human in biting another; indeed, so can human teeth. Does this justify the preemptive removal of either? Yes, hens do have a natural tendency to peck one another, while humans are generally not inclined to bite one another. Still, hens have managed to survive each other's pecking since time immemorial, leading to the creation of the phrase "pecking order," so demonized in the above passage as something dangerous and frightening. Indeed, how could any such order— a word that implies the organization of living beings into some form, however primitive, of a society— have ever emerged if the natural result of this practice was death?

Webster's Dictionary defines humane as "marked by compassion, sympathy, or consideration for humans or [nonhuman] animals." Raising a cow outdoors, then murdering said cow, shows neither compassion nor sympathy, nor consideration for that cow at all; ultimately the cow is murdered, and in that instant, any compassion we may have demonstrated to the cow previously evaporates. A switch is flicked, and we shift from being concerned about the cow's wellbeing (hence raising them outside so that they can enjoy freedom of movement, sunshine, camaraderie with other cows, and so forth) to having absolutely zero regard for the same cow's wellbeing by voluntarily ending their life. As it is impossible to consume beef without murdering a cow, therefore, there is simply no such thing as a humane burger or a humane steak.

"Okay, we get it, you're vegan— bully for you!" you cry from the bleachers. "But what was that you said about strawberries…?" We cannot assume a strawberry is humane for the same reasons we cannot assume it is cruelty-free solely from the knowledge that it is a strawberry. Driscoll's berry purveyors are a prime example of how even plant-based foods can be the result of exploitation (please visit boycottsakumaberries.com and join Familias Unidas por la Justicia[22] and hundreds of farmers and food justice advocates worldwide in boycotting Driscoll's). "Humane" and "cruelty-free" are buzzwords that go hand-in-hand in an effort to comfort consumers and dissuade them from asking too many questions.

I know; it sounds hopeless, doesn't it? Shall we all voluntarily starve to death? Of course not. The best advice I can offer for those who strive to truly eat humanely is to pay close attention to where your food is sourced from and who is doing the sourcing. As much as possible, we should also support small farmers and grow some food ourselves so as to minimize our reliance on corporate food structures which so commonly violate the rights of their workers. We can't be perfect in an imperfect world, but we can commit ourselves fully to walking the path of least harm.

Sustainable: The push for sustainability as it relates to food is mainly concerned with whether current food practices around the world can withstand the test of time, and be utilized just as they are being utilized now for the indefinite future. In order to form an opinion on this matter, one must first determine: Sustainable for whom?

Are we talking about sustainable for the planet— can the planet survive the system? Do we mean humans? Nonhumans? Specific humans, such as those with a certain income, of a certain race, or in a certain climate?

One example of a wholly unsustainable food system that dominates much of the world presently is animal agriculture (see "Animal Agriculture: An Injustice to Humans and Nonhumans Alike," beginning on Page 85). The resources used by this system are being used at such fast rates that it cannot be sustained; the planet will simply run out— of land for grazing, water for bred nonhumans (and us humans) to drink, and breathable air, as greenhouse gas emissions run through the roof and global warming takes hold (See Dawn Moncrief's "Natural Resource and Food Sovereignty Benefits of Plant-Based Diets," beginning on Page 107). This is also not sustainable from the perspective of nonhuman animals who are being "farmed" (exploited and/or murdered). Finally, it is not sustainable for wildlife, who not only require air and water, as we do, but who are also habitually culled or otherwise driven off of their rightful land so that humans can build more ranches. Even "humane" farming, independent of the nonhuman animal perspective, is unsustainable, owing to its egregious land use and impact on wildlife.

We must address the need to think beyond simple lifestyle changes— though those are certainly helpful in the short term— and consider radically changing where and how we live in order to create a truly sustainable future.

Citations

1. Gayeton, Douglas. LOCAL: The New Face of Food and Farming in America. *New York: Harper Design*, June 2014.

2. Ibid.

3. "Definition of Food Security." Published by the United States Department of Agriculture's Economic Research Service. Accessed January 15, 2018.

4. "The Lexicon of Sustainability: Food Terms." Published by PBS.Org. February 5, 2014.

5. "Permaculture Ethics." Published by PermaculturePrinciples.Com. Accessed January 15, 2018.

6. "Permaculture Design Principles." Published by PermaculturePrinciples.Com. Accessed January 15, 2018.

7. "Seed Bank." Wikipedia. Accessed January 15, 2018.

8. "Biodiversity." Wildlife Guide. Published by the National Wildlife Federation. Accessed January 15, 2018.

9. O'Keefe, Brian. "Inside Big Chocolate's Child Labor Problem." *Fortune.Com*, March 1, 2016.

10. "Columbian Exchange." Wikipedia. Accessed January 15, 2018.

11. Philpott, Tom. "How Mexico's Iconic Flatbread Went Industrial and Lost Its Flavor." *Grist.Com*, September 14,

2006.

12. DePalma, Anthony. "How a Tortilla Empire was Built on Favoritism." *The New York Times*, February 15, 1996.

13. Ross, John. "The Plot against Mexican Corn." *Counter-Punch.Org*, February 14, 2007.

14. "The Impact of Fair Trade Certification." Published by Fair Trade Certified. Accessed January 15, 2018.

15. "About Fair Wild." FairWild.Org

16. Bittman, Mark. "A Walk on the Wild (Edibles) Side." *The New York Times*, July 9, 2015.

17. "Food Deserts." Published by Food Empowerment Project. Accessed January 15, 2018.

18. "Food Justice." LexiconofFood.Com, accessed January 18, 2018.

19. Gayeton, Douglas. LOCAL: The New Face of Food and Farming in America. *Harper Design*, June 2014.

20. "Frequently Asked Questions." Published by CertifiedHumane.Org. Accessed January 15, 2018.

21. Ibid.

22. "Who We Are." Published by Familias Unidas por la Justicia. Accessed January 15, 2018.

CHAPTER ONE

Food Waste, Feeding Bans, and the Criminalization of Dissent

By Saryta Rodríguez

The Numbers

The United States Environmental Protection Agency (EPA) defines food waste in the United States as "uneaten food and food preparation wastes from residences and commercial establishments such as grocery stores, restaurants, and produce stands, institutional cafeterias and kitchens, and industrial sources like employee lunchrooms."[1] As of July 2016, approximately fifty percent of all produce in the United States was thrown away annually,[2] while the USDA's Economic Research Service currently estimates that approximately thirty to forty percent of the total US food supply is wasted annually.[3] This amounts to approximately $160 billion dollars in food, with a carbon footprint of 3.3 billion tons of carbon equivalent. [4]

Globally, about one third of all food that is grown— roughly 1.3 billion tons of food— is thrown away annually.[5] A 2014 report from the Food and Agriculture Organization of the United Nations (FAO) notes that food waste also results in water waste— the equivalent of *three times* the size of Lake Geneva[6], a massive lake on the north side of the Alps with a water volume of approximately 89 cubic kilometers[7]— or this many gallons: 23,510,000,000,000. Again, it's that much water *times three* being wasted: **70,530,000,000,000 gallons**!

While one might presume that more food would be wasted in wealthier parts of the country while less food would be wasted in lower-income states, the opposite has proven to be the case. The percentage of meals wasted is highest in Kentucky, Tennessee, Mississippi and Alabama (East South Central), as well as in a vertical strip of the Western United States spanning north-to-south from Montana to New Mexico and west-to-east from Nevada to Colorado— notably excluding all three states on the West Coast.[8]

Grocery waste follows a similar pattern but stretches further east of Kentucky to include Virginia and the Carolinas; as well as further north, including Michigan and Wisconsin. The highest percentage of *restaurant* meal waste specifically is highest not in a coastal culinary mecca, such as New York or San Francisco, or even in the up-and-coming Southern culinary hub of Atlanta, but rather in the poorest state in the Union: Mississippi.[9] These findings indicate that food waste is not merely a question of the Haves versus the Have-Nots, but is symptomatic of a deeper cultural problem that crosses class boundaries (as well as nationwide policies that keep the prices of certain goods artificially low).

One of many contributing factors to food waste in the United States is the implementation of federal farm subsidies. These subsidies encourage farmers to a) specialize in a few commodity crops rather than a diversity of produce and b) expand, growing more and more food even as the costs of the commodity crops drops.[10] (Corn-, soybean-, and wheat-growing operations are the clearest example of these subsidies at work.)

Farmers face penalties for not providing "dependable volumes" of crops to their buyers, regardless of both current supply of each crop in the U.S. and uncontrollable growth factors such as weather, which leads to overplanting. Not only does this result in food waste, but it also yields myriad environmental damages, such as contaminated water from fertilizer runoff.[11]

We as consumers are also largely to blame for the food waste epidemic plaguing the United States. Consumers are less likely to purchase bruised, oddly-shaped or otherwise "unattractive" produce. Grocery stores and consumers alike tend to throw away food two or three days before its Sell By date: consumers out of fear that the food will make them sick, grocery stores in preemption this fear— knowing that consumers will likely not purchase any items so close to the Sell By date and that these items will end up being thrown away in a few days, anyway.[12]

The Bright Side

Thankfully, there is a plethora of organizations and initiatives currently operating with the goal of minimizing food waste in the U.S. One such organization is Food Not Bombs, a national network of kitchens held together by a commitment to both the minimizing of waste and to veganism. This organization collects food that is perfectly edible yet would otherwise be thrown away because it is approaching expiration or is simply unattractive from grocery stores and other places. Volunteers then prepare vegan meals with these items and distribute the meals in public squares to anyone who is hungry, independent of age, race, socioeconomic status, or any other demographic factor.

Unfortunately, due to another of Food Not Bombs' core values— *cookhouse autonomy*, or the right of each individual kitchen to operate in its own way, without national oversight— some branches of Food Not Bombs have abandoned their commitment to veganism in recent years. However, veganism remains an essential founding principle of the organization, as stipulated by founder Keith McHenry, and most cookhouses still adhere to it.

Keith McHenry, who is also the author of *Hungry for Peace: How You Can Help End Poverty and War with Food Not Bombs,*[13] rightly acknowledges the inherent connection between justice for humans and justice for nonhumans in the text of the very first of Food Not Bombs' three founding principles:

We want our food to reflect our dedication to nonviolence, and that includes violence against all beings, including animals. *We only prepare food that is strictly from* *plant sources so people will always know and trust Food Not Bombs that our food is safe and nonviolent. At times, we do get donations of dairy and meat products and redirect them to soup kitchens that aren't vegetarian because we believe eating is more important than being politically pure; however, we NEVER cook with animal products ourselves and only share breads that might have dairy when it is not possible to know for sure.*[14]

If you are interested in working with Food Not Bombs, visit www.FoodNotBombs.Net and find a kitchen near you— but please do inquire ahead as to whether or not your nearest kitchen still adheres to the First Principle of Food Not Bombs, as otherwise it is perpetuating the age-old myth that humans are more important than nonhumans and that it is acceptable for a "justice" organization to help perpetuate violence against the latter. Ethical consistency matters, and I find it most unfortunate that some kitchens have chosen to lean on the Second Principle, cookhouse autonomy, as a loophole through which to violate the first.

If there is no Food not Bombs kitchen near you, no worries; the website also provides detailed instructions on how to start your own!

Chilis on Wheels (www.ChilisOnWheels.Org) is a smaller nonprofit organization based in Brooklyn, New York, that also feeds hungry humans with vegan food with chapters across the mainland US and Puerto Rico. Founder Michelle Carrera has also opened a food distribution center in Puerto Rico named "Casa Vegana de la Comunidad" under the Chilis on Wheels – Puerto Rico chapter after actively helping Puerto Ricans in need in the aftermath of Hurricane Maria, which devastated the island and many others in the Caribbean in September 2017.

In the Washington, D.C. area, Fuel the People, founded by Starr Baker, is also employing vegan food and products to combat hunger. Starr explained, "Through distributing plant-based lunches across the city and conducting research along the way, we aim to make a statement about the current state of food justice and food insecurity in DC."

Another company leading the way against food waste, Hungry Harvest, contributes to the fight against food waste by rescuing produce that is not being purchased strictly for aesthetic reasons, such as an unusual shape or color, and selling it at a discount directly to consumers. Consumers can place an order through www.HungryHarvest.Net and have it delivered right to their door. Hungry Harvest, founded in 2014, sparked a wave of similar companies into existence, such as Imperfect Produce (www.ImperfectProduce.Com), which was founded the following year.

Some grocery stores have also recently shown initiative to combat food waste. The East of England Co-op, a grocery store chain in the U.K., announced in December 2017 that it now sells products that are up to a month past their "best before" dates in all of its 125 outlets, with prices reduced to just ten pence, or about 13 cents. Roger Grosvenor, joint chief executive at the East of England Co-op, said in a statement:

The vast majority of our customers understand they are fine to eat and appreciate the opportunity to make a significant saving on some of their favorite products. This is not a moneymaking exercise, but a sensible move to reduce food waste and keep edible food in the food chain. By selling perfectly edible food we can save 50,000 items every year that would otherwise have gone to waste.[15]

According to the U.K.'s Food Standards Agency, the U.K. throws away nearly 8 million tons of food and drink each year, with its manufacturing and retail sector wasting an additional 2 million tons.[16] East of England anticipates that its new program will save more than two tons of food waste annually.[17]

In the U.K., unlike Use By dates, which denote an official safety standard— "eating this food after this date may result in discomfort or even illness"— Best Before dates are more about quality control.[18] For instance, eating a slice of bread after its Best Before date won't make you ill, but the bread might be stale and not taste as good or have as enjoyable a texture as it would have if you'd eaten it before the Best Before date.

In the United States, we encounter one of three phrases on our food quite often: Use By, Best Before and Sell By. Best Before is the same as in the U.K., while Use By is the very last date recommended for food *quality* but is still not a safety standard. In other words, U.S. American Use By dates do not indicate that food eaten after that date will make you sick— except when they are found on infant formula. Sell By, which doesn't exist in the U.K., tells U.S. American stores how long to keep items on shelves, and is, again, *not a safety indicator*. So, in all three cases, as long as we are not talking about infant formula, it is safe to eat these foods past the date given.[19]

Initiatives like this price-reducing model employed by

the East of England Co-op could be employed in the United States and other places in an effort to combat hunger. If you are interested in starting this type of scheme in your area, why not start by advocating to your local grocery store to take this step?

Challenges and Threats to Our Success

Creative solutions and initiatives such as those referenced above inspire hope that the current, dire situation can still be reversed. Unfortunately, at the same time, ongoing legal initiatives and funding deficits pose direct challenges to the success of some of these well-meaning and much-needed organizations. For instance, on September 16, 2015, the Obama administration set an ambitious goal: to reduce food waste in the U.S. by 50% by the year 2030.[20] Unfortunately, one year later, funding the initiative remained an issue. Battle Creek, a town in southern Michigan, made a request in June 2016 seeking a grant from the Department of Agriculture to help it raise $3 million to build composting and waste-to-energy facilities, as well as launch consumer campaigns in an effort to reduce the amount of food that ends up in the town's landfills. As of September 12th of that year, they had not heard back. With just a few months left in the administration's lifetime, no funding mechanism had been put in place to support initiatives aimed at achieving the 2030 food waste reduction goal.[21]

In May of 2017, during the fifth month of the Trump administration's tenure, it was announced that the EPA would be scrapping food waste efforts from the EPA's budget, further decimating the U.S.'s ability to rise to Obama's "Food Waste Challenge."[22]

To make matters worse, an October 2014 report by the National Coalition for the Homeless found that twenty-two cities had successfully passed "feeding bans"— laws that outright criminalize food donation.[23] A *Mother Jones* article reported that "Most of these measures regulate public property use, especially parks, by either requiring permits to share food on public property or banning the practice altogether."[24] In so doing, "feeding bans" have made organizations such as Food Not Bombs, which rely on public squares for food distribution, illegal.

In 2011, over twenty activists in Orlando, Florida were arrested for feeding approximately thirty-five people in need in a public park. In 2014, ninety-year-old World War II veteran Arnold Abbott was arrested in Fort Lauderdale for feeding the homeless, while the previous year, church members in Raleigh, North Carolina were threatened with arrest for regularly distributing food to the needy on weekend mornings.[25]

Michael Stoops, director of community organizing at the National Coalition for the Homeless, said: "They don't want the homeless in the downtown areas. It interferes with business. Cities have grown tired of the problem, so they think by criminalizing homelessness they'll get rid of the visible homeless populations." Susan Dunn, the legal director of the South Carolina chapter of the American Civil Liberties Union (ACLU), has also pointed out that another common way of criminalizing anti-hunger work beyond the Public Property Use excuse— alleged concerns about food safety, prompting the requirement of members of charitable organizations to get food handling permits before distributing food— clearly target those trying to feed the homeless because they are never used to prosecute or penalize, say, relatives at family reunions.[26]

These "feeding bans" or "food-sharing bans," in one form or another, are currently in effect in the following cities across the U.S.[27] (Note: This list may not be exhaustive.):

Chico, California
Costa Mesa, California
Hayward, California
Pasadena, California
Daytona Beach, Florida
Lake Worth, Florida
St. Petersburg, Florida
Lafayette, Indiana
St. Louis, Missouri
Manchester, New Hampshire
Charlotte, North Carolina
Raleigh, North Carolina
Shawnee, Oklahoma
Medford, Oregon
Harrisburg, Pennsylvania
Columbia, South Carolina
Myrtle Beach, South Carolina
Houston, Texas
Salt Lake City, Utah
Olympia, Washington
Seattle, Washington

This disturbing trend runs parallel to the broader criminalization of dissent currently taking place under the Trump administration. In July 2017, over 155 demonstrators were arrested at Senate office buildings after exercising their constitutional right to protest attempts to repeal the

Affordable Care Act.[28] In September of that same year, the Department of Justice demanded that Facebook turn over account information for "anti-administration activists."[29] In March 2018, two activists were arrested for simply standing outside of the gates of the U.S. Department of the Treasury and reading a letter challenging U.S. Secretary of the Treasury Steve Mnuchin about his budget proposal.

The repeal of the U.S. American net neutrality rules that took place in December 2017[30] further jeopardizes lawful political dissent by enabling broadband service providers to manipulate how quickly or slowly websites load— or whether or not they load at all. This may well result in pro-administration propaganda becoming widely accessible while information that challenges or threatens the current administration in any way, such as critiques of its policies or calls to action via protest or petition, are systematically suppressed.

Aside from the criminalization of *assisting* the homeless (and of dissenting against unjust policies), homelessness itself is being increasingly "discouraged"— penalized—in a wide variety of ways. Laws such as those against loitering have long criminalized homelessness, forcing the homeless to take such measures as sitting at bus stops for long periods of time (so that, if harassed by law enforcement, they can claim that they were simply waiting for the bus) or spending what little money they have to get on subway trains and ride them back and forth for hours at a time. However, now even seemingly apolitical systems inherent to the structure of a given city, such as architectural design, are being manipulated and utilized to punish those without a home. Architectural features that have been increasingly installed in cities around the world in the past five years to discourage the presence of homeless people include park benches with a third armrest in the middle, preventing people from laying down on them; and spikes rising from sidewalks and areas in front of buildings, preventing people from sitting in those spaces.[31]

Now more than ever, it is critical that each and every one of us take a stand to defend not only our individual rights to free speech and peaceful protest, but also our collective right as a community to support one another through charitable actions such as food distribution.

What YOU Can Do to Combat Food Waste:

- **When dining out, don't order more than you can eat.** If you do, take your leftovers home for a later-meal or tomorrow-meal. If you're not a fan of reheating leftovers, take them with you anyway and give them to someone in need.

- **Don't be afraid of "ugly" produce.** It tastes the same, and contains all of the same nutrients, as its prettier counterpart. I promise.

- **Don't freak out about Sell By or Best Before dates.** Take the time to learn what spoiled or rotten food looks, smells and feels like, and let *those* be your guide to whether or not something is edible.

- **Support organizations and businesses that combat food waste**— with time (volunteering), money (donations) and/or promotion (spreading the word of their existence).

- **If you live in a city where "food-sharing bans" are in effect**: Contact your congresspeople. Rally your neighbors! Circulate petitions! Organize a local demonstration! Let elected officials know that *they will lose their seats if they continue to criminalize charity.* Conversely, reach out to congresspeople in your area who are actively fighting these bans and let them know that they have your support— and, if they keep up the good work, they can count on your vote in the future.

Citations

1. "Terms of Environment: Glossary, Abbreviations and Acronyms (Glossary F)." United States Environmental Protection Agency, 2006.

2. Goldberg, Suzanne. "Half of All U.S. Food Produce is Thrown Away, New Research Suggests." *The Guardian,* July 13, 2016.

3. "U.S. Food Waste Challenge FAQ." U.S. Department of Agriculture.

4. Sengupta, Somini. "How Much Food Do We Waste? Probably More Than You Think." *The New York Times,* December 12, 2017.

5. Ibid.

6. "Food Wastage Footprint: Impacts on Natural Resources." Food and Agriculture Organization of the United Nations Summary Report, 2013.

7. "Lake Geneva." Wikipedia. Accessed June 18, 2018.

8. Goldberg, Eleanor. "These States Waste the Most Groceries and Restaurant Meals." *The Huffington Post,* August 15, 2016.

9. Ibid.

10. "Subsidizing Waste: How Inefficient U.S. Farm Policy Costs Taxpayers, Businesses, and Farmers Billions." Union of Concerned Scientists Report, 2016.

11. Gupta, Kamayani. "Farm to Landfill: The Cost of Food Waste in America." *The Huffington Post*, August 30, 2016.

12. Ibid.

13. McHenry, Keith. "Keith McHenry: Artist, Author, Chef and Organizer." Accessed December 17, 2017.

14. Food Not Bombs Official Website. Accessed December 17, 2017.

15. Wamsley, Laurel. "To Cut Waste, U.K. Grocery Chain Will Sell Products Past 'Best Before' Date." *NPR.Org*, December 4, 2017.

16. Food Standards Agency Official Website. Accessed December 17, 2017.

17. Wamsley, Laurel. "To Cut Waste, U.K. Grocery Chain Will Sell Products Past 'Best Before' Date." *NPR.Org*, December 4, 2017.

18. "Use By and Best Before Dates." Food Standards Agency, Accessed April 18, 2018.

19. "Food Product Dating." US Department of Agriculture. Accessed April 18, 2018.

20. Aubrey, Allison. "It's Time To Get Serious About Reducing Food Waste, Feds Say." *NPR.Org*, September 16, 2015.

21. Hopkinson, Jenny. "USDA Food Waste Funding

Scarce a Year After Setting Goal." *Politico,* September 12, 2016.

22. EPA's Spending Cut Plan, produced March 21, 2017. Official documents accessed via *The Washington Post.*

23. "Share No More: The Criminalization of Efforts to Feed People in Need." National Coalition for the Homeless Report, October 2014.

24. Levintova, Hannah. "Is Giving Food to the Homeless Illegal in Your City, Too?" *Mother Jones*, November 13, 2014.

25. Ibid.

26. Ibid.

27. "Share No More: The Criminalization of Efforts to Feed People in Need." National Coalition for the Homeless Report, October 2014.

28. Williams, Clarence. "Police Arrest 155 Health Care Protesters at U.S. Capitol." *The Washington Post,* July 19, 2017.

29. Schneider, Jessica. "D.O.J. Demands Facebook Information from 'Anti-Administration Activists.'" *CNN.Com,* September 30, 2017.

30. Kang, Cecelia. "F.C.C. Repeals Net Neutrality Rules." *The New York Times*, December 14, 2017.

31. Rosenberger, Robert. "How Cities Use Design to Drive

Homeless People Away." *The Atlantic*, June 19, 2014.

CHAPTER TWO

Animal Agriculture: An Injustice to Humans and Nonhumans Alike

By Saryta Rodríguez

It may come as a surprise to some of you that a book about food justice should include a critical analysis of the impact of animal agriculture on our planet, fellow creatures, ourselves, and each other. Indeed, many organizations seem to consider these topics divorced, or perhaps in direct competition with one another. Some promote veganism as an ethical necessity while neglecting to address the tangible realities of human hunger, income disparity, or the systemic racism that results in a preponderance of food swamps in neighborhoods of color, while all of the "good" grocery stores are in white, or mostly-white, neighborhoods here in the US.

One also commonly encounters the reverse:

organizations and initiatives that promise to aid the poorest and hungriest among us humans, with absolutely zero regard for the role of nonhuman animals in this process—no mention, even, of how animal agriculture in fact *hinders* the feeding of humans, much less the inescapable reality that animal agriculture is fundamentally unethical, habitually robbing innocent creatures of their autonomy, their families and their lives.

I have come to understand, as a food justice worker first, and then later as a vegan, that it is in fact not only *useful* to discuss animal agriculture when attempting to promote food justice worldwide; it is *essential.* To attempt to solve the problem of a lack of food justice without taking into consideration the detrimental impacts of animal agriculture on us, others, and the planet is like trying to understand how cancer spreads without knowing anything about cell growth.

One of the many ways in which animal agriculture hinders food justice on a global scale is via appropriation of valuable resources that can otherwise be used to feed human beings. Animal agriculture actually uses up significantly more human-friendly food than it produces. Feed Conversion Ratios, or FCRs, measure the amount of feed crops used to produce one "unit of meat" (in reality, one part of a nonhuman animal's body which a human can regrettably choose to consume— against the nonhuman's will, of course). They can be found by dividing a nonhuman animal's food intake with their average daily weight gain.[1]

I won't bore you with all of the available data on this, but here are some quick facts on animal agriculture's use of resources:

- The FCR for cow flesh, or "beef," ranges in the US from 4.5-7.5 according to a 2013 report.[2] This means that, according to this source at least, it can take anywhere from **four to nearly eight times as much weight** in edible, natural human food, such as grains and corn, to produce one consumable "unit" of cow flesh.

- Other sources paint an even more dismal picture. While *Beef Magazine*, among others, claim the ratio is six-to-one using *live weight*— the total weight of the cow when he or she is alive— in their conversions,[3] when one uses *edible weight* (which excludes bone, skin and other non-edible parts of a creature), the ratio becomes **twenty-five-to-one**.[4] That's an astounding *twenty-five times* as much edible human food being used to produce just *one* unit of someone else's flesh for humans to needlessly consume.

It's worth noting that the primary issue regarding world hunger is not that there is a lack of food to go around. As other essays in this book, such as "Food Waste, Feeding Bans and the Criminalization of Dissent," attest, the issue is primarily that food is being improperly distributed and inefficiently used (one example: according to a report by the UNEP— United Nations Environmental Programme— about one-third of all food produced worldwide is lost or wasted[5]). So, while we might be able, already, to feed many more people than we currently are by being less wasteful and more efficient in our practices, the fact of the matter is we could easily feed *thousands more* by moving beyond animal agriculture, an ancient and long-respected tradition that has nevertheless failed us and continues to do so.

Nonhuman animals currently enslaved by animal agriculture account for approximately thirty percent of the Earth's total land mass.[6] The global human population is expected to reach over nine and a half billion by 2050,[7] and global meat consumption is expected to increase annually *at least* through 2024.[8] According to A Well-Fed World, a nonprofit organization based in Washington D.C. devoted to solving world hunger through a vegan praxis, it is estimated that we will need two-thirds more land than the Earth actually possesses in order to meet predicted demand for animal flesh and byproducts over the next twenty-five years.[9]

Imagine, for a moment, what could be done with that 30% of all usable land *right now* to address hunger and improve food sovereignty! The land on which cows, chickens, pigs and other nonhumans who will inevitably be murdered in the name of "food" could be used instead to grow even more food for hungry humans— in some cases, anyway. In others, such as the 80% of all Amazon rainforest destruction resulting from demand for nonhuman animal farmland,[10] this land could be rehabilitated so as to continue to serve its original purpose— housing and feeding the many nonhumans native to the region, who are being displaced, starved and in many cases rendered extinct by our unwarranted interference in their homes. While creatures such as the Great Short-Tailed Bat have already gone extinct due to deforestation, these represent only one-fifth of the total number of species expected to go extinct in the coming years.[11]

When we think about veganism and begin to challenge animal agriculture as the default method of human food production, we often hear about the plight of the farmed animal victims themselves— pigs, cows, chickens, and others. In reality, the pool of victims of animal agriculture runs much deeper; not only are hungry humans around the world victims of this gross mismanagement of resources, but also nonhumans we consider to be "wild," untamed or un-enslaved directly by humans.

This is one of many reasons that "humane farming"— the practice of providing nonhuman animals with ample living space, sunlight, food and other amenities prior to their murder— falls short. This position is ethically unsound and insufficient, but it is also impractical to think that we could ever possibly provide every single farmed animal on the planet with that much space *without taking space away from wild creatures*, who are equally entitled to autonomy and safety.

One example of the threat posed to wild nonhumans by the farming of domesticated nonhumans is the case of the Yellowstone Bison. Over the past decade, Yellowstone Park has been legally mandated to send hundreds of bison to their deaths because nearby ranchers are concerned the bison could infect their "cattle"— enslaved cows— with a disease called brucellosis, which causes mother cows to abort their young, impacting the supply of bodies ranchers can eventually sell as "food."[12] Cows and calves on ranches aren't allowed to die of diseases; they are supposed to remain healthy so that they can be murdered, and their corpses sold for profit. Thus, other species trying to survive also fall victim to ensure maximized profits.

One popular question that arises among non-vegans when animal agriculture's use of land is mentioned is, "Well, the animals have to live somewhere, anyway—where would they live instead? And how would that be any better?" Similar questions arise when discussing the environmental impact of animal agriculture, as we will shortly. The most important thing to understand in this regard is that many— perhaps even *most*— of the cows, pigs, chickens and other farmed animals that exist today exist because they were bred. In other words, they were brought into this world unnaturally for the explicit purpose of feeding us humans. Were animal agriculture to be put to bed, breeding rates for all of these animals would surely drop, and eventually we would see a radical decrease in the total population of each.

For those who remain, the best option in terms of housing and security would be *sanctuaries:* places funded by donations and grants, where nonhuman animals are allowed to live without being exploited. Beyond the obvious ethical advantages of raising nonhumans at a sanctuary—such as that they will not be injected with hormones, not be confined to cages and never, ever be murdered— sanctuaries are advantageous in that they do not pack as many nonhumans onto their property as possible. Naturally, animal farms have an incentive to raise as many creatures on their property as possible, so as to make more money. This results in higher concentrations of methane and other harmful nonhuman animal (non-edible) byproducts than at a sanctuary, where the priority is not maximizing the *quantity* of nonhuman animals raised but providing each with the best possible quality of life.

"Climate Change is a Hunger Risk Multiplier"[13]

According to a United Nations report released in 2010, animal agriculture, due to the greenhouse gases emitted by "livestock," or enslaved cows and other farmed creatures,[14] is among the foremost contributors to climate change—wreaking more havoc on our environment than all forms of transportation worldwide combined.[15] In fact, some argue that our understanding of animal agriculture's massive contribution to climate change is severely underestimated due to calculation parameters and discrepancies. For instance, Livestock's Long Shadow,[16] a report released by the Food and Agriculture Organization (FAO), suggests that animal agriculture accounts for only 18% of greenhouse gas emissions, whereas other sources— such as Livestock and Climate Change,[17] released by World Watch— assert that it is actually responsible for 51% of all greenhouse gas emissions.

The fact of the matter is that US "cattle" ranchers had a monopoly on space, with an astonishing *788 million acres* of land suitable for agriculture (excluding Alaska) devoted to raising cattle in the 48 continental states— out of a total of 1.9 billion acres of land. In other words, just over 41% of land that is suitable for food production in the continental US is devoted exclusively to cattle grazing.[18] Aside from the greenhouse gases resulting therefrom, USDA Wildlife Services kills millions of wild animals annually so as to protect the interests of ranchers. In 2014, Wildlife Services murdered over 2.7 million wild animals,[19] including:

- 796 bobcats
- 61,702 coyotes

- 305 mountain lions
- 15,911 prairie dogs
- 8,971 common ravens
- 1,001 feral/free ranging dogs and cats
- 22,416 beavers
- 570 black bears
- 322 gray wolves, and
- 2,930 foxes

Not only is this a hideous injustice against all of these creatures, but where predators are concerned, it is not even necessarily the solution to "livestock loss"— actual carnivores eating nonhuman animals that we humans want to eat ourselves. A 2014 study examining livestock data from 1897 through 2012 found that lethal force against wolves actually increased the odds of a wolf attack on sheep by 4 percent and cows by 5 to 6 percent. This is likely owing to the fact that killing wolves causes the pack structure to collapse, which results in solitary wolves looking for food beyond their usual hunting grounds.

"Wildlife Services once again wasted taxpayer dollars killing nearly three million animals last year," Oregon Representative Peter DeFazio, a Democrat, told VICE News. "Their lethal predator control program is particularly inhumane and totally unnecessary."[20]

The exceptional amount of clout cattle ranchers have in the US is further exemplified by their ability to occupy nearly 200,000 acres of space in Oregon[21] for several weeks in protest of new grazing fees without being arrested or fined, while Black Lives Matter activists are habitually arrested and threatened with egregious fines for holding a miniscule fraction of that space for just a handful of hours.[22]

Animal agriculture also has a devastating impact on water quality, threatening an already increasingly scarce global water supply by contributing to water pollution via "...animal wastes, antibiotics and hormones, chemicals from tanneries, fertilizers and pesticides used to spray feed crops."[23]

As the World Food Programme and similar institutions attest, climate change is a hunger risk multiplier. Climate change leads to drought and other catastrophes in communities that are already suffering from lack of food sovereignty. Some of the poorest nations in the world are being increasingly devastated by droughts, floods, storms and other natural disasters. In 2007, according to a World Watch Institute report, potato crops in Bolivia were devastated by drought; Hurricane Felix destroyed crops in Honduras and Guatemala; and floods in Tabasco, Mexico caused over $700 million in food-supply-related damages. An official with the Tabasco Economic Industry was quoted as saying, "One hundred percent of all the crops and agricultural fields have been lost because of flooding," which drove up prices nationwide and put one third of Tabasco residents out of work.[24]

While as usual, the poorest of the poor are the ones most impacted by these things, climate change is no longer just an issue for brown-people-way-over-*there*; its affects can now be felt right here in rich, techy, mostly-white, privileged California, as evidenced by the severe drought we've been experiencing since 2012 and which Governor Jerry Brown officially declared a State of Emergency in January 2015.[25]

War, Theft, and Other Human Follies

Warfare also poses a major threat to food sovereignty and food security. While the mainstream Animal Rights Movement here in the U.S., and even those who identify as members of the Animal Liberation Movement (who draw an important distinction between improving nonhuman animal *welfare* and demanding nonhuman animal *liberty*), continue to celebrate Israel as a "vegan" nation, because it provides its soldiers with nonhuman-animal-by-product-free boots and other clothing items to wear while trampling on Palestinian villages and farms, Palestinians are making great strides towards embracing veganism and nonhuman liberation— but, egregiously, their access to natural vegan foods such as fruits, vegetables and grains is being increasingly threatened[26] and even outright denied[27] under Israeli occupation.

This is just one of many examples of how war threatens food sovereignty and in so doing, not only disadvantages human populations but also nonhuman populations, as humans have less and less of a choice with respect to what they eat, rendering it more likely for them to feed themselves at the expense of nonhumans. Meanwhile, an oppressor's ability to make ethical food choices (from a nonhuman perspective) within its oppressive regime should not excuse it from atrocities it commits as an oppressor against humans.

Restoring our ecosystem to its natural state of balance is essential in order to achieve global food sovereignty, and this is simply not possible under the current Animal Agriculture regime. Every life, human or nonhuman, has not only inherent value but also at least one inherent function— a naturally occurring benefit it bestows upon the planet. The most obvious example of this, perhaps, is the bee, without whose pollination scores of crops necessary for human survival would perish. We need to support, rather than oppress, our fellow creatures in these endeavors.

Some bee populations are currently severely threatened by, among others, two distinctly human interventions in their affairs: exposure to pollen contaminated with fungicides[28] and our blatant theft of their food supply— the honey they produce— and replacement of it with high fructose corn syrup, which wreaks havoc on their immune system.[29] In the past five years, thirty percent of the US bee population has disappeared,[30] while currently *thirty-four species of bee* are classified by the Xerces Society for Invertebrate Conservation as Imperiled, Critically Imperiled, or Possibly Extinct.[31]

There is, of course, a difference between bees that are native (wild) and commercially used/exploited bees (used for crops, as pollinators). It is important not to conflate the two, as they face different threats: honeys actually contribute to the decline of wild bees. The conservation status of bees, therefore, does not relate to honeybees as, in the U.S., they are a non-native species contributing to the decline of wild pollinators.

Feeding Us While Respecting Them

One of the greatest misnomers currently plaguing the food justice movement is the notion that one must ultimately choose between feeding humans and respecting nonhuman autonomy in order to proceed. The truth is that myriad organizations have already made great strides in both directions simultaneously, and continue to do so. The following organizations and initiatives confirm on a daily basis that yes, it *is* possible to feed hungry humans without oppressing or slaughtering nonhumans:

Grow Where You Are

The Grow Where You Are collective was founded in 2012 by dynamic husband and wife duo Eugene Cooke and JoVonna Johnson-Cooke. Grow Where You Are partners with organizations and individuals to bring food abundance to various communities, with a special focus on veganic farming. Members of Grow Where You Are "design, install and maintain multiple public and private spaces where food is produced using agroecological principles. [They] have been training residents in this dynamic form of urban agriculture for over ten years."[32]

Among Grow Where You Are's numerous achievements in the field of food sovereignty are:

- The creation of the Good Shepherd Agroecology Center in Atlanta's historic West End;
- The completed development of a "robust three-acre farm-to-market site" that has produced over 15,000 pounds of food and served over 8,000 people; and
- The ongoing development of the Awali Veganic Homestead Education Center near Stone Mountain, Georgia, which hosts veganic workshops, community feasts and an organic seed library.

Grow Where You Are also offers online consultations

and garden design services,[33] and is currently organizing Atlanta's premiere veganic CSA (Community Supported Agriculture) in midtown Atlanta.[34]

Grow Where You Are believes in veganic farming not only due to the cruel exploitation of nonhuman animals inherent in animal agriculture, but also due to its staunch commitment to sustainability, which Eugene and JoVonna will address directly later in this book. Some basic planetary health reasons that Grow Where You Are rejects animal agriculture include its contributions to greenhouse gases, species extinction, ocean dead zones, and habitat destruction.[35]

To get involved, visit www.growwhereyouare.farm and click on More → Contact to send a message, or Consultations to book a consultation. You can also find and follow Grow Where You Are on Facebook.

A Well-Fed World

A Well-Fed World's motto is "Feeding Families, Saving Animals."[36] This non-profit organization, based in Washington D.C., hosts myriad programs all over the world aimed at feeding the hungry without exploiting our nonhuman brethren.

One such program is called **Plants-4-Hunger.** You may have already heard of initiatives such as Heifer International's "gift-pig" program, and others like it, in which folks are encouraged to donate funds with which a nonhuman animal can be sent to a needy family to help feed that family— independent of the profound negative impact this will inevitable have on the pig, cow or goat's life; on the human family's health; and on the overall wellbeing of our planet. Plants-4-Hunger responds to these well-meaning yet misguided programs by soliciting donations with which to "support on-the-ground, animal-free hunger relief projects."[37]

Four projects funded via Plants-4-Hunger are:

- *The International Fund for Africa's School Lunch Program* in Ethiopia, which aside from providing daily assistance to hungry children also develops income-generating bakeries and food-generating community gardens.
- *Karen's Nutrition Program* in Guatemala, which seeks to improve nutrition among impoverished children. As part of this program, local women's groups produce enough baked goods and soymilk to distribute to 400 children.
- *Vegan Society for Protection and Care of Animals's (VSPCA's) Vegan Meals for the Poor Program* in India, which serves food on Mondays, Wednesday and Fridays— days on which recipients do not receive food assistance from any other program.
- *Grow Where You Are*, discussed above.

Aside from providing hands-on hunger relief through a vegan praxis, A Well-Fed World also strives to raise awareness about food justice issues from both the human and nonhuman perspective. For instance, its Film for Thought outreach campaign awards grants for cutting-edge food justice video projects, employs social media to extend the reach of these videos, provides ample resources for those endeavoring to make a food justice film, and even donates portable DVD players to those who wish to engage in Pay-

Per-View advocacy: a modern form of advocacy in which advocates offer members of the public $1 to watch a three-to-five-minute film about a pressing social issue.

To get involved, visit awfw.org and sign up for A Well-Fed World's monthly newsletter. You can also find and follow the organization on Facebook.

Food Empowerment Project

Food Empowerment Project is an incredible organization founded by lauren Ornelas (who prefers her name to be typed lowercase) in 2006, which makes the connection between human, nonhuman and environmental injustices and works tirelessly to expose and correct them. Food Empowerment Project wears many hats:

- It is a human rights initiative, bringing to light injustices in the food system occurring globally, such as the atrocities that the chocolate industry commits against children on the Ivory Coast and in other parts of the world[38] and the plight of produce farmers from Mexico and the Southern United States;[39]

- It is a vegan advocacy initiative, empowering folks to go vegan by sharing information on the many problems with animal agriculture, delicious recipes that span various cultures (including a sister website devoted specifically to vegan Mexican cuisine, VeganMexicanFood.Com), and by emphasizing the various cruelties committed against slaughterhouse laborers[40] and other human victims of the nonhuman-animal-based food complex; and

- It is an intersectional justice collaborative, habitually exploring issues of sexism and racism within the mainstream animal rights movement here in the US and demanding an increase in cultural sensitivity and elimination of stereotyping, tokenization and microaggression against nonhuman animal advocates of color, women, and those of us who do not fit into the gender binary.

Just one of the many essential resources that the Food Empowerment Project provides to anyone wishing to eat more ethically is a Recommended Chocolate List.[41] Food Empowerment Project researched and reached out to many of the world's leading chocolate providers to demand where their chocolate comes from, and based on that extensive research they developed a list, available through their website as well as in the form of a smart phone app, of chocolate they have confirmed is ethically-sourced—meaning that, among other things, children were not "purchased" or kidnapped from their homes, locked in at night, denied education or viciously beaten in order to produce this delicious-yet-wholly-unnecessary food for privileged Westerners to consume.[42]

On a personal note, lauren is a true inspiration to me—a fantastic speaker, intelligent and powerful, yet also remarkably approachable. When I first started to engage in nonhuman animal advocacy in the Bay, I encountered more than a fair bit of resistance in my attempts to bring seemingly "unrelated" or "distracting" topics, such as the Black Lives Matter Movement and demonstrations in Baltimore in the Spring of 2015, into the conversation. Her advice was invaluable to me and has helped me not only to stand up for myself and be confident in advocacy situations, but also to do the same in my personal life. She reminded me that, all politics aside, I deserve to be treated well, and to be heard.

To get involved, visit www.foodispower.org, sign up for their newsletter, or go to Get Active → Volunteer to view a brief list of volunteer opportunities. You can also find the Food Empowerment Project on Facebook and email the group directly at info@foodispower.org.

In closing, it is my hope that more organizations like these will continue to take root around the world in a way that is inclusive of both human and nonhuman issues. I invite activists to consider taking a further major step when contacting these organizations. You can help spread these initiatives by starting chapters in your local community or by approaching established food justice organizations in an effort to help them recognize that oppressions are interconnected and there is no reason to oppress one marginalized group over the other when working towards justice.

Citations

1. "Simple Calculations: Feed Conversion, Daily Gain and Mortality." *The Pig Site,* April 3, 2014.

2. Shike, Dan W. "Beef Cattle Feed Efficiency." Driftless Region Beef Conference 2013. Accessed December 17, 2017.

3. Reuter, Ryan. "Supplement Conversion Ratio." *Beef Magazine*, November 3, 2009.

4. *Poultry Production Manual*, published by the University of Kentucky College of Agriculture, Food and the Environment. Accessed December 17, 2017.

5. "One Third of All Food Wasted!" United Nations Regional Information Centre for Western Europe. Accessed February 28, 2018.

6. Spear, Stefanie. "Cowspiracy Exposes the Truth about Animal Agriculture." *EcoWatch*, October 10, 2014.

7. "World Population Projected to Reach 9.6 Billion by 2050." United Nations Report, June 13, 2013.

8. "Meat Market: A History of U.S. Meat Consumption." *AgWeb.Com,* accessed December 17, 2017.

9. Capps, Ashley. "7 Ways Plant Foods are Fighting Global Hunger." *AWFW.Org*, October 29, 2015.

10. Spear, Stefanie. "Cowspiracy Exposes the Truth about Animal Agriculture." *EcoWatch*, October 10, 2014.

11. Sample, Ian. "Amazon's Doomed Species Set to Pay Deforestation's 'Extinction Debt.'" *The Guardian*, July 12, 2012.

12. Hegyi, Nate. "Yellowstone Bison Release Launches Criminal Investigation." *NPR.org,* January 27, 2018.

13. Egal, Florence. "Climate Change, Food Security and Nutrition." *FAO.Org*, April 17, 2015.

14. Vrbicek, Andy. "The World's Leading Driver of Climate Change: Animal Agriculture." *NewHarvest.Org*, January 18, 2015.

15. "Global Greenhouse Gas Emissions Data." *EPA.Gov*, accessed December 17, 2017.

16. "Livestock's Long Shadow: Environmental Issues and Options." Food and Agriculture Organization of the United Nations, 2006.

17. Goodland, Robert. Anhang, Jeff. "Livestock and Climate Change." *WorldWatch.Org*, November/December 2009 issue.

18. Wuerthner, George. "The Truth about Land Use in the United States." *WesternWatersheds.Org*, Summer 2002. Vol. IX, No. 2.

19. Messenger, Stephen. "2.7 Million Creatures Killed Last Year in U.S.'s Secretive War on Animals." *The Dodo,* April 14, 2015.

20. Dattaro, Laura. "The Federal Government Killed Nearly 3 Million Animals Last Year." *VICE News*, April 14, 2015.

21. House, Kelly. "Oregon Standoff Leaders Urge Local Ranchers to Defy Feds on Grazing Fees." *Oregon Live,* February 23, 2016.

22. Black Lives Matter. "BART Directors: When it comes to ending the war on Black communities, which side are you on?" Petition accessed via ColorofChange.Org, December 17, 2017.

23. "Rearing Cattle Produces More Greenhouse Gases Than Driving Cars, UN Report Warns." *UN.Org,* November 29, 2006.

24. "Worldwatch Perspective: Rebuilding Food Security is Essential in Wake of Natural Disaster." *WorldWatch.Org,* accessed December 17, 2017.

25. "California Drought Crisis." *CBSNews.Com,* accessed December 17, 2017.

26. Aldabbour, Belal. "Israel Spraying Toxins over Palestinian Crops in Gaza." *Al Jazeera*, January 19, 2016.

27. Associated Press, Jerusalem. "Israel Used 'Calorie Count' to Limit Gaza Food during Blockade, Critics Claim." *The Guardian,* October 17, 2012.

28. Hagopian, Joachim. "Death and Extinction of the Bees." *Global Research*, November 8, 2017.

29. Philpott, Tom. "First We Fed Bees High-Fructose Corn Syrup, Now We've Given Them a Killer Virus?" *Mother Jones*, February 5, 2014.

30. Hagopian, Joachim. "Death and Extinction of the Bees." *Global Research*, November 8, 2017.

31. "Red List of Bees: Native Bees in Decline." Xerces Society for Invertebrate Conservation, accessed December 17, 2017.

32. "About." *GrowWhereYouAre.Farm*, accessed December 17, 2017.

33. "Consultations." *GrowWhereYouAre.Farm*, accessed December 17, 2017.

34. "Veganic CSA." *GrowWhereYouAre.Farm*, accessed December 17, 2017.

35. "Veganic Growing." *GrowWhereYouAre.Farm*, accessed December 17, 2017.

36. A Well-Fed World Official Website, accessed December 17, 2017.

37. "Gifts." *AWFW.Org*, accessed December 17, 2017.

38. "Child Labor and Slavery in the Chocolate Industry." *FoodisPower.Org*, accessed December 17, 2017.

39. "Produce Workers." *FoodisPower.Org*, accessed December 17, 2017.

40. "Slaughterhouse Workers." *FoodIsPower.Org*, accessed December 17, 2017.

41. Food Empowerment Project's Official Chocolate List.

42. Gregory, Amanda. "Chocolate and Child Slavery: Say No to Human Trafficking This Holiday Season." *The Huffington Post*, October 31, 2013. Updated December 6, 2017.

CHAPTER THREE

Natural Resource and Food Sovereignty Benefits of Plant-Based Diets

By Dawn Moncrief

Food justice and food security discourses are increasingly informed by food sovereignty insights and values. In their ideal state, each of these frameworks prioritizes universal access to safe, nutritious, and culturally appropriate foods. However, food sovereignty goes further by also focusing on where food comes from, how it is produced, and who benefits. Food sovereignty prioritizes the needs of people, local control, community health, environmental protection, and food as a right over corporate, political, and foreign interests.[1]

In our globalized world, respecting food sovereignty and independence does not equate to a *laissez-faire*, hands-off approach to the needs of other countries or abdicating responsibility for the impact of our personal choices and policies. To the contrary, since our global food system is highly interconnected, food sovereignty— even in remote locations— can be bolstered by improving food consumption and production patterns at the local, national, and international levels. Practices that are less depleting of our shared and finite natural resources are of particular importance from a food sovereignty perspective.

With these factors in mind, this chapter highlights the ways in which food sovereignty— especially for the world's poorest and most vulnerable populations— is advanced by prioritizing policies and behaviors that favor plant-based food consumption and production. In particular, the focus is on how shifting away from resource-intensive animal-sourced foods (meat, dairy, and eggs) increases food access and sustainability by directly utilizing crops for human consumption and conserving scarce resources.

Animals: Inefficient Food Converters

A key reason that rearing animals for food is an inefficient and wasteful use of natural resources is that *farmed animals eat much more food than they produce.*[2] Using animals for food also requires vast amounts of land, water, and energy to house, hydrate, and eventually process their bodies and secretions into edible commodities. While statistics vary about how dire the consequences are when using animals for food, the overarching theme of massive resource depletion, pollution, and greenhouse gas emissions is generally consistent.

In order to better appreciate the scale of inefficiency in

using animals for food, it is helpful to consider their feed conversion ratios (FCRs). Generally speaking, FCRs refer to the amount of feed crops needed to produce a unit of live weight gain per animal… or unit of edible food.

Reported ratios vary widely depending on the factors included in their calculation (breed, age, geography, method of production, feed composition, etc). Beyond that, however, key to understanding FCRs is to be mindful of the distinction between live weight, carcass weight, and edible weight. For our purposes here, we'll focus on live weight (the most conservative ratios) and edible weight (the most accurate ratios).

Live weight FCRs, which yield lower ratios that downplay inefficiencies, are used in agribusiness publications. These numbers are often cited by others who share the industry's priorities, want to err on the conservative side, or don't understand their nuances.[3] What is important for consumers, researchers, and policymakers is the edible weight. *Edible weight FCRs* more accurately illustrate the extreme inefficiencies of animal-sourced foods. These much higher feed-to-food ratios represent the ready-to-consume products after slaughter and processing (removing bones, blood, and other inedible parts).

Widespread pro-meat bias results in a more cavalier attitude by the public and policymakers toward standard feed-related crop loss than other types of crop loss. For example, there is widespread outcry against food loss due to waste or biofuels. A UN official went so far as to call biofuels a "crime against humanity" and a "catastrophe" for the poor.[4]

However, when conservative estimates indicate that half of food crops are lost in the production of chicken meat, chicken is celebrated for its efficiency. Note that chicken's 2:1 feed-to-food ratio is the *live weight FCR*, which underestimates the *edible weight FCR* by about half. The inefficiencies of mammals are even greater, with pigs exceeding a 9:1 edible weight FCR, and beef cows averaging 25:1.[5] To be clear, this means that cows eat 25 times more food than they produce – *which is about triple the commonly reported live weight ratios.*[6]

To make matters worse, these ratios only consider concentrated feed crops and do not include all sources of caloric intake. Livestock[7] proponents sometimes make the case that farmed animals can graze on forage (such as grass) and roughage (such as hay) that is unfit for humans. However, grazing is just less concentrated feed and it still has significant land-use and environmental opportunity costs. When calculations consider forage and roughage calorie sources, the inefficiencies of animal-sourced foods skyrocket.[8]

Consider that it's not just billions of animals benignly eating abundantly available grass on otherwise non-arable land that has no other uses. Grazing uses vast amounts of land– much of it arable– that could grow food for people directly, grow crops for biofuels, be reforested to increase photosynthesis, or be used for a variety of other purposes that increase the social good instead of diminish it.

Grazing is also far from benign when considering the higher methane emissions that emanate from grass-fed ruminant animals (cows, goats, sheep), and the loss of photosynthesis to absorb greenhouse gases that results from land clearing and deforestation to create grazing pastures. Grass-fed ruminants emit up to four times more methane than when fed concentrated grains.[9] This is especially important because methane is an extremely potent greenhouse gas. Over a 100-year time-frame, methane is up to 25 times stronger than carbon dioxide (CO_2). Given the urgency of slowing climate change, however, a more condensed time-frame is appropriate. When basing calculations over 20 years, the Intergovernmental Panel on Climate Change (IPCC) now puts the global warming potential (GWP) of methane at 84 times more powerful than CO_2.[10]

Conserving Resources: Land, Water, and Energy

Regardless of production method, with 70+ billion land-based farmed animals reared for food annually,[11] their inherent inefficiencies have immense global impact. According to the widely cited "Livestock's Long Shadow" report by the Food and Agricultural Organization of the United Nations (FAO), livestock use approximately a third of the earth's land surface, mostly permanent pasture, but also including a third of the global arable land used for feed.

The FAO report acknowledges that the livestock sector is a major driver of deforestation as "forests are cleared to create new pastures...especially in Latin America where, for example, some 70 percent of former forests in the Amazon have been turned over to grazing."[12] The International Livestock Research Institute reports even higher numbers, concluding that "livestock systems occupy 45% of the global surface area."[13] The World Resources Institute reports that globally, "more than twice as many hectares of land are used for grazing by livestock as are used for the production of all crops combined."[14]

These extremely high land-use figures maintain despite utilizing the most confining, space-limiting factory farming methods for two-thirds of the world's farmed animals.[15] In industrialized countries, the percentage of animals intensively confined is much higher, and intensive confinement is the primary method for dealing with the drastic global increases in animal-sourced food production.

The FAO further estimates that by 2025, 64% of the world's population will be living in water-stressed regions. According to water scientists, consumption of animal products already contributes to more than 25% of humanity's water footprint.[16] In the United States, the livestock industry accounts for nearly half of all the nation's freshwater use.[17]

A water footprint is calculated using a *life-cycle analysis* to measure the amount of water used across the various stages of the production chain. In total, producing one pound of animal-based protein takes as much as 100 times the amount of water needed to produce one pound of grain-based protein.[18] Roughly 98% of animal products' water footprint is derived from feed irrigation (concentrates and roughage),[19] but water is also needed for billions of animals to drink, to clean millions of gallons of blood and waste every day from farms and slaughterhouses, and to "process" animal carcasses into packaged edible meat.[20]

In addition to dangerously high levels of water (mis)use, the livestock industry also accounts for nearly 30% of worldwide water pollution.[21] Sources include fertilizers and pesticides used on feed crops, antibiotics and hormones given to animals, and *billions* of tons of untreated animal manure and waste annually. In the U.S. alone, farmed animals produce 1.37 billion tons of solid waste every year (130 times more than human waste, which is treated).[22] Throughout the world, massive amounts of manure are sprayed into the air, spread on crops, or stored in underground holding tanks (euphemistically called "lagoons"). While often uncritically lauded as fertilizer, the reality is that the excessive quantity of animal waste is a toxic contaminant that overwhelms and poisons local and global ecosystems.

A life-cycle analysis also provides details about the considerable number of energy-based inputs and processes required for animal-sourced foods. According to David and Marcia Pimentel, as reported in the *American Society for Clinical Nutrition*, it takes 11 times more fossil fuel to produce one calorie of animal protein than to produce one calorie of plant protein.[23] More than half of the fossil fuel use in the livestock sector derives from the production of feed crops, including the chemical fertilizers used on corn and soy feed crop monocultures.[24] Additionally, vast amounts of fossil fuels are required for on-farm temperature regulation, waste treatment, animal transport, slaughterhouse operations, storage, refrigeration, and retail distribution.[25]

The Impact of Food Choice on Food Sovereignty

The crop-intensive and resource-intensive nature of the livestock industry exacerbates many food sovereignty concerns. As our population expands and animal-sourced food production surges,[26] demand for diminishing natural resources will continue to undermine local control and access to food. This is especially detrimental for the world's poor, resulting in increased disparities, deprivation, and death from undernourishment and hunger-related causes.

Competition for limited resources is also a source of violent social strife. According to a recent sustainability report, "High meat consumption causes social conflicts and aggravates the problem of hunger...Competition for scarce land and between 'food and fodder' is proving to be dramatic for global nutrition."[27]

From a food sovereignty perspective, it is also important to note the connections between high levels of animal-sourced food consumption and "land grabs," or more specifically "meat grabs."[28] Livestock-driven land grabs are a growing phenomenon in which small-scale farmers and entire communities are forced off their property in order for multinational corporations to raise farmed animals or grow feed crops, generally for export or for wealthier domestic populations. In Paraguay, for example, more than 100,000 farmers have been expelled to make room for the industrialized production of soy-based feed crops since 1990.[29]

To further compound the injustice, two-thirds of agriculture-based land grabs are in countries with high levels of hunger. While many land grabs are transacted under the guise of decreasing local hunger, more than 60% of crops grown on foreign-controlled land are exported.[30]

Similarly, industrialized farms and feed operations infiltrate countries with lax regulations. These powerful "meat regimes" pollute host communities, undermine subsistence farmers, and abuse local people with harsh and dangerous labor practices.[31] Proliferation of these foreign-owned and/or export-oriented firms is increasingly common.

With or without trade agreements, collaborations between national and foreign power-holders increase wealth for elites in both countries at the expense of vulnerable, marginalized communities. As the report "Developing the Meat Grab" notes, "the expansion of industrial meat production on a world scale including its voracious appetite for land and water is also the erosion of food securities and sovereignties, and an important form of dispossession concerning not only land, but also the relationships between people and agroecosystems."[32]

Conclusion

Numerous reports confirm that shifting towards plant-based diets would increase the world's supply of available calories. The United Nations Environmental Programme (UNEP), in particular, calculated that enough crops for an additional 3.5 billion people could be saved by consuming plants directly instead of feeding them to livestock.[33] With better understanding of the immensity of crops and natural resources unnecessarily used to produce animal-sourced foods, the food sovereignty discourse would be well-served by reframing meat and other animal products as forms of overconsumption, redistribution, and waste.

Unfortunately, while the case for shifting away from animal-sourced foods domestically and internationally is exceptionally strong, there is resistance among some within the food sovereignty movement. The same is true for the broader food movement and beyond, but opportunities still abound for widespread improvements by rethinking entrenched biases for animal-sourced foods and centering solutions on plant-based food and farming systems. Eliminating animal-sourced food consumption and production would not automatically ensure food sovereignty, but strategies to achieve food sovereignty would be greatly improved by global shifts toward plant-based food and farming.

Thus, the recommendation that follows for high-income and/or high-consuming populations with access to plant-sourced foods is to minimize (ideally eliminate) consumption of animal-sourced foods as an act of global responsibility and in solidarity with those who have less social, economic, and political power. The recommendation for less-affluent populations is to prioritize increasing the availability of nutrient-rich, plant-sourced foods, while also working to minimize (ideally eliminate) consumption of animal-sourced foods. This shift to plant-centered food production and consumption is a practical approach to increasing food supply, control, and access that not only conserves natural resources but also puts downward pressure on food prices.[34] This combination of environmental protection and decreased food prices both reduces acute hunger and improves food security more broadly to create a healthier, well-fed world for all.

Citations

1. Holt-Giménez, Eric, "Food Security, Food Justice, or Food Sovereignty" Food First Backgrounder based on "Food crises, food regimes and food movements: rumblings of reform or tides of transformation?" *Journal of Peasant Studies* 38:1, 2011 pp.109-144.

2. "Scarcity vs. Distribution." *A Well-Fed World.* Accessed May 1, 2018.

3. Raines, Dr. Christopher R. "The Butcher Kept Your Meat?" Penn State University. Accessed May 1, 2018.

4. Lederer, Edith, "UN Expert Calls Biofuel 'Crime Against Humanity,'" *LiveScience.* October 27, 2007.

5. University of Kentucky: College of Agriculture, Food and Environment, *Poultry Production Manual.* March 25, 2014 (accessed May 15, 2016).

6. A Well-Fed World, "Feed:Meat Ratios" Webpage, accessed May 29, 2016.

7. The term "livestock" is controversial among animal advocates. It is used here as it is common in food security and environmental research, and because "livestock industry" covers the full range of land-based animal use (including but not limited to factory farms). While the term "animal agribusiness" is accurate, it leans euphemistic and does not as adequately convey the harsh realities of the industry. While not covered here, the use of fish and other aquatic animals is highly problematic and includes many of the same problems since farmed fishing also uses

feed.

8. Searchinger, Tim et al, "Creating a Sustainable Food Future: A menu of solutions to sustainably feed more than 9 billion people by 2050." World Resources Institute, United Nations, and World Bank, December 2013.

9. Harper, L. A., et al, "Direct measurements of methane emissions from grazing and feedlot cattle," *Journal of Animal Science* 77:6,1999 pp. 1392-1401.

10. Stocker, T.F. et al, *Climate Change 2013: The Physical Science Basis. Contribution of Working Group I to the Fifth Assessment Report of the Intergovernmental Panel on Climate Change,* Cambridge University Press, Ch. 8, 2013 pp. 714.

11. Compassion in World Farming, "Strategic Plan 2013-2017: For Kinder, Fairer Farming Worldwide." 2013, pp. 3.

12. Steinfeld, Henning, et al, "Livestock's Long Shadow: Environmental Issues and Options." Food and Agriculture Organization of the United Nations, and the Livestock Environment and Development Initiative, November 2006.

13. Thornton, Philip, Mario Herrero, and Polly Ericksen. "Livestock and Climate Change," *Livestock Exchange.* International Livestock Research Institute, November, 2011.

14. Ranganathan, Janet et al. "Shifting Diets for a Sustainable Food Future." World Resources Institute. Washington, DC. April, 2016.

15. Compassion in World Farming, "Strategic Plan 2013-2017: For Kinder, Fairer Farming Worldwide." 2013 pp. 3.

16. Mekonnen, M. and A. Hoekstra, "A Global Assessment of the Water Footprint of Farm Animal Products," *Ecosystems* 15, 2012. pp. 408.

17. Steinfeld, Henning et al, "Livestock's Long Shadow: Environmental Issues and Options." Food and Agriculture Organization of the United Nations, and the Livestock Environment and Development Initiative, Ch.4, November 2006.

18. Pimentel, David and Marcia Pimentel, "Sustainability of meat-based and plant-based diets and the environment," *American Society for Clinical Nutrition.* 2003. pp.662s.

19. Hoekstra, Arjen Y., "The Hidden Water Resource Use Behind Meat and Dairy," *Animal Frontiers* 2:2 2012, pp. 5.

20. Steinfeld, Henning et al, "Livestock's Long Shadow: Environmental Issues and Options." Food and Agriculture Organization of the United Nations, and the Livestock Environment and Development Initiative, Ch.4, November 2006.

21. Mekonnen, M. and A. Hoekstra, "A Global Assessment of the Water Footprint of Farm Animal Products," *Ecosystems* 15, 2012. pp. 408-9.

22. Pew Commission on Industrial Farm Animal Production citing U.S. Environmental Protection Association

(EPA). Webpage accessed May 28, 2016.

23. Pimentel, David and Marcia Pimentel, "Sustainability of meat-based and plant-based diets and the environment." *American Society for Clinical Nutrition* v.123 2003. pp.661-662.

24. Steinfeld, Henning et al, "Livestock's Long Shadow: Environmental Issues and Options." Food and Agriculture Organization of the United Nations, and the Livestock Environment and Development Initiative, November 2006, pp. 89.

25. Food and Agricultural Organization of the United Nations, "Framework for calculating fossil fuel use in livestock systems." Accessed May 22, 2016.

26. Meat production is predicted to more than double from 2000 to 2050 due to high per capita rates in high-income countries combined with high growth rates in emerging economies (known as the Livestock Revolution). This term was coined by Delgado, Christopher et al. "Livestock to 2020: The Next Food Revolution." International Food Policy Research Institute, Food and Agricultural Organization of the United Nations, and International Livestock Research Institute, 1999._. See also: A Well-Fed World— www.awfw.org/livestock-revolution

27. Stoll-Kleemann, Susanne and Tim O'Riordan. "The Sustainability Challenges of Our Meat and Dairy Diets." *Environment: Science and Policy for Sustainable Development*, 57:3, pp. 34-48, DOI: 10.1080/00139157.2015.1025644. p.40-41.

28. Schneider, Mindi. "Developing the meat grab," *Journal of Peasant Studies.* June 17, 2014.

29. Stoll-Kleemann, Susanne and Tim O'Riordan. "The Sustainability Challenges of Our Meat and Dairy Diets." *Environment: Science and Policy for Sustainable Development,* 57:3, pp. 34-48, DOI: 10.1080/00139157.2015.1025644. pp.40-41.

30. Oxfam, "Our Land, Our Lives: Time out on the global land rush." Briefing Note. October 2012. pp.6.

31. Nierenberg, Danielle. "Factory Farming in the Developing World." *World Watch Magazine.* May/June 2003. V.17, No.3.

32. Schneider, Mindi. "Developing the meat grab." *Journal of Peasant Studies.* June 17, 2014. pp.1.

33. Nellemann, C., et al. 2009. *The environmental food crisis – The environment's role in averting future food crises.* United Nations Environmental Programme: UNEP Rapid Response Assessment. February 2009. pp. 27.

34. Westhoff, Patrick. *The Economics of Food: How Feeding and Fueling the Planet Affects Food Prices.* Peason Education, FT Press, 2010. pp. 97.

CHAPTER FOUR

Case Study and Interview: Occupy the Farm

By Saryta Rodríguez and Gustavo Oliviera

An ongoing grassroots movement focused on land sovereignty, Occupy the Farm, came to be in the fall of 2011. The movement has since become an integral example of community-driven direct action in service of the advancement of land rights movements.

Land rights philosophy has long centered the notion of moving away from large-scale, monocultural, industrial food production (of which there are myriad operations that in fact primarily produce animal feed for nonhuman animal farming) and towards small-scale, diverse, community-led production. The 2007 Nyéléni World Forum on Food Sovereignty Declaration called for "integral agrarian reform that guarantees peasants full rights to land," and demanded that such reform ensure "respect for local autonomy and governance."[1] This ideology, coupled with the success of such movements as Brazil's Landless Workers' Movement (MST)—one of the largest social movements in Latin America, with an estimated informal membership of 1.5 million people[2]— has "inspired many others to see land occupations as a hopeful tactic for achieving land access."[3]

The Landless Workers' Movement was born through a process of occupying *latifundios* (large, landed estates) and officially became a national movement in 1984. The movement has led to over 2,500 land occupations and resulted in the reclamation of 7.5 million hectares of previously unproductive land for farming purposes. Families who now live and farm on this land continue to advocate for better education, credit for agricultural production and cooperatives, and access to health care through MST.[4] The MST occupations have resulted not only in successful settlement of this land but also in the gaining of *legal titles* to the land[5]— though it is worth noting that the movement maintains it is already, immediately entitled to occupy any unproductive land (with or without the granting of any titles), owing to a section in Brazil's most recent Constitution (1988) that states land should fulfill a social function.[6] MST also notes that, based on 1996 census statistics, 3% of the Brazilian population owns two-thirds of all "arable" (farmable) land in Brazil.[7]

The notion of *land sovereignty* has been evolving to draw a distinction between *access to* and *ownership of* land. This newer framework seeks to bypass the dichotomy between the institutional lens of property rights (that land ownership is a matter of legality) and the populist lens (that land ownership is a matter of "local control") and focus instead on the practical matter of how land is used and who is allowed to use it— independent of who "owns" it.[8] Antonio Roman-Alcalá, director of the Agroecology Organizing Project, writes:

Though conditions of farmers and farmer movements and the national cultural politics of land do not seem conducive to 'radical' land action or national land reform, occupations are found to still have a potential contribution, insofar as they contest property norms, construct agrarian subjectivities, and improve movement capacity.[9]

Although the struggle for food sovereignty is a global one, there are certain differences in the challenges faced in "the North" (such as Western Europe, Canada and the United States) and in "the South" (such as Central and South America), and these regions have different representation. The best-known food sovereignty organization worldwide is La Via Campesina, which has member coalitions from every continent save Antarctica.[10] La Via Campesina's 2016 organizational brochure summarized the group's goals and structure as follows:

La Via Campesina is an international movement bringing together millions of peasants, small- and medium-size farmers, landless people, rural women and youth, indigenous people, migrants and agricultural workers from around the world.

Built on a strong sense of unity and solidarity between these groups, it defends peasant agriculture for food sovereignty as a way to promote social justice and dignity and strongly opposes corporate-driven agriculture that destroys social relations and nature.

Women play a crucial role in La Via Campesina. The movement defends their rights and gender equality. It struggles against all forms of violence against women. Young farmers also play a very important role as an inspiring force in the movement. La Via Campesina comprises of 164 local and national organizations in 73 countries from Africa, Asia, Europe and the Americas. Altogether it represents about 200 million farmers. It is an autonomous, pluralist, multicultural movement, political in its demand for social justice while being independent from any political party, economic or other type of affiliation.[11]

While ideology and shared goals (such as autonomy and ecological health) unite the globe in the fight for food sovereignty, shifts in strategy— such as the aforementioned evolution of land sovereignty theory— are required in order to take into account variations in context. Alcalá warns that, "uncritical emulation of tactics of Southern members of the FS movement may prove strategically detrimental to the long-term success of FS activism in the North."[12] ("FS" therein referring to "food sovereignty.") The ideal of democracy, for instance, remains ever elusive as race-, class-, and gender-based discrimination influence who is and is not granted access to the decision-making table. The role of capitalism in exacerbating inequality can also not be understated; this, too, makes achieving the food sovereignty ideal of egalitarianism at best difficult, and at worst impossible, to achieve. In an editorial contribution for *The Journal of Peasant Studies,* global food policy expert and research professor Raj Patel succinctly described a key issue of this movement:

To make the right to shape food policy meaningful is to require that everyone be able substantively to engage with those policies. But the prerequisites for this are a society in which the equality-distorting effects of sexism, patriarchy, racism, and class power have been eradicated. Egalitarianism, then, is not something that happens as a consequence of the politics of food sovereignty. It is a prerequisite to have the democratic conversation about food policy in the first place.[13]

The Road to Occupy the Farm

As the owners of the land that would become occupied and lead to a land rights protest and movement known as Occupy the Farm, University of California Berkeley's role in the occupation was heavily influenced by context and preexisting relationships. The context of UC Berkeley at the time of Occupy the Farm was doubtlessly influenced by the fact that, for decades preceding the movement, a group of scholars at the university "frequently challenged many of the dominant themes of contemporary agricultural research" and "organized curricula questioning the assumptions of conventional agriculture and its sciences while encouraging the development of alternative agricultural practices based on principles of ecology."[14] This critique had "stimulated an intellectual climate calling forth a scrutiny of the university's role in the production of knowledge and the social consequences of its works."[15]

The Division of Biological Control at UC Berkeley has, since the 1960s, argued for processes that achieved common agricultural goals, such as pest control, while respecting the balance of the ecosystem— such as introducing natural predators to these pests, rather than employing dangerous chemical pesticides to do the job. The group also opposed monocultures on the grounds that these result in "ecological settings that are inhospitable to a variety of insects, including natural predators."[16] Unsurprisingly, these positions ran afoul of Big Ag's practices— namely, the use of monocultures and pesticides— and to say that agribusiness was "unenthusiastic" about the Berkeley group's findings is an understatement. Thus, before the specific subject of *land use* by the university came under a microscope, the relationship between agricultural researchers at the university and mainstream agricultural institutions was already a contentious one.

Robert Van den Bosch took things one step further than his colleagues previously had by publishing *The Pesticide Conspiracy* in 1978, which criticized both agribusiness's practices and the complacency of the university itself:

> *By and large, the aggie colleges and their associated experiment station and extension services are social anachronisms that view their mission as one narrowly oriented to crop production and agri-business and hardly concerned with broader societal interests. What else explains their virtual neglect of the concerns of the farm worker, the consumer, the urban homemaker, and the environmentalist? This narrowness is perhaps explainable in largely agricultural states, where the universities are dominated by farming interests.*[17]

Translation: The university had a social responsibility to not only ensure that the agricultural practices it engaged in were ecologically sound, but also that the humans involved— "the farm worker, the consumer, the urban homemaker"— were all treated justly. Its role was not simply to produce "good science," but rather to ensure justice for members of the community it inhabited— and from which it profited. It is through this lens, then, that Occupy the Farm must be considered, as the land that was occupied during this movement technically "belonged" to UC Berkeley.

A Food Sovereignty Movement Grows in Berkeley

Under what became known as the Occupy the Farm (OTF) movement, food sovereignty activists occupied the Gill Tract (GT), land owned by UC Berkeley, in order to "broaden food sovereignty's land access considerations beyond the South, and to analyze conditions where political actions (including occupations) can help achieve changes in land access regimes."[18] The group mobilized on Earth Day (April 22), 2012. Hundreds of people showed up, broke the locks to the GT's gates, occupied the land, and planted vegetables on it. After police showed up, plants were destroyed, and arrests were made, many returned repeatedly to harvest crops from the remaining plants and distribute thousands of pounds of food to low-income residents of the region.

In 1928, the Gill family sold its 104-acre parcel of land in Albany, California to UC Berkeley for the purposes of agricultural research. It was used in this manner by UCB's Division of Biological Control until the division lost funding in the 1990s, after which the university began to sell off portions of the land and repurpose other portions for housing. In 1997, an environmental coalition in the Bay Area proposed that the remaining Gill Tract be used for urban and sustainable farming education and research. The proposal was briefly considered, but ultimately rejected. In 2004, the university approved a plan to turn the remaining GT into market-rate housing, grocery stores and baseball fields— a move which was fiercely rejected by urban farming organizations, Albany residents, students and community groups. Nevertheless, by 2011, development seemed imminent. Thus, Occupy the Farm was born.[19]

In the end, the results were mixed. In September 2012, a referendum by Albany residents forced their city council to rescind approval of a development agreement that had been made for the northern portion of Gill Tract; however, the southern portion of the tract was still slated for development, and so OTF continued to organize. It hosted a boycott against Sprouts supermarket, the tenant that was to replace Whole Foods on the southern tract after the latter pulled out as a result of the city council's rescission; and made several attempts at guerilla planting, resulting in another round of arrests. Finally, in July of 2013, a small section of the north side of Gill Tract was offered for a "community-based" agroecology project. This land was later dubbed the "Gill Tract Community Farm," and managed via "collaborative governance" among OTF members, Albany residents, students, and faculty. The notion of acquiring the *entire* tract for these purposes was thus summarily dismissed.[20] However, the movement did not entirely end there but continued to pursue an educational approach to radicalism and provide training in direct action to community members, in addition to continuing to grow, harvest and distribute food to those in need.

An In-Depth Look at OTF with Gustavo Oliveira

UC Berkeley alumni and Occupy the Farm (OTF) spokesperson, Gustavo Oliviera, is a long-time Food Movement activist that has worked with both La Via Campesina and MST. I first met Gustavo in December of 2015 during the People's Harvest Forum in San Francisco, California. The forum was hosted by Millahcayotl (now Seed the Commons), an organization founded by Nassim Nobari and Chema Hernández Gil. Its aim closely mirrored that of this book: to unite people from environmental, farmers' rights, and nonhuman rights perspectives and career paths to discuss food justice more broadly and find ways in which we could all come together to ensure that future generations have regular access to healthful, sustainable, plant-based foods, while the individuals growing this food are both treated and compensated justly. Although the event brought to light the obvious divisiveness between the vegan community and proponents of farmers' rights— despite both movements having many of the same goals, including justice, environmental awareness, and food security— I was able to learn about OTF. As we will learn from Gustavo, the occupation-based movement continues to this very day:

SR: How did your interest in food sovereignty struggles first develop? What were some of your earliest experiences working directly in this realm of food justice or food sovereignty, or what you sometimes refer to as the Food Movement?

GO: *Well, I was raised in Brazil, and while I did not have an agricultural background after my parents' generation, not since back to my grandparents' generation, I was studying politics, social justice, democracy, and things like that. I realized there is no solution to crises in Brazil— whether it was crime or poverty or social inequality or environmental devastation, whatever it was— without first addressing the fundamental inequality of land distribution, which could be traced back to colonization. We have an extremely modern agribusiness sector, literally built on colonial plantations and patterns of land distribution. This began for me as an academic interest, and I soon realized that agrarian reform was essential. I looked into these things a bit while pursuing my bachelor's degree, but I really dug deeper while attaining my master's degree at the University of Colorado-Boulder. Afterwards, I* *took a gap year and went back to Brazil, where I was lucky to be able to become involved with the Landless Rural Worker's Movement of Brazil, (Movimento dos Trabalhadores Rurais Sem Terra – MST). I wanted to learn firsthand about land redistribution and agrarian reform, and to become involved, in a more hands-on way, with the issues I had studied.*

I was lucky that they saw my genuine desire to participate in this struggle, and that they were able to help me be productive and of use. The MST is very prominent internationally, so they host many social movement organizers and scholar-activists from abroad, who require translation and interpretation. And the MST also sends several of its own organizers abroad and require translation of their own documents and communiques for international distribution. They do a lot of international relations work because they have always understood that their struggle is a global one: capitalism is global, peasants and workers everywhere are struggling against the same transnational corporations, so the MST pursued international collaborations for a long time. Especially since the 1990s and the struggle against the WTO's Agreement on Agriculture, which led to the creation of La Via Campesina (as an international umbrella of rural social movements). Therefore, the MST needed translators, and I was lucky they recruited me to become a translator for Via Campesina and the MST for that year. It was a great experience for me, as I learned a lot. Then I had the chance to come back to the States to pursue a PhD at UC Berkeley in geography and political ecology, and I wanted to work on land struggles in Brazil and globalization. It was through this collaboration with the MST that I determined my research questions and project. The MST also invited me to join the national coordination for Friends of MST, a group of people from Northern regions, such as the United States, who support MST by organizing human rights campaigns, hosting MST visitors when they came to visit the North, fundraising, and other things like this. I also got pretty involved in our student movement and graduate student labor union at UC Berkeley, which led directly to my involvement in the Occupy Movement at Berkeley and Oakland. So, when Occupy the Farm sprung up and they reached out to me, it really resonated with both my passion and experience.

I think it is worth noting, though, that even though I had a somewhat urban childhood, I was lucky enough to have a large backyard garden, with eight beds measuring about one yard by four yards each, full of vegetables. We also had an orchard with about ten different fruit trees, and we even raised about a dozen chickens for a few years. So even then, at a young age and in an urban setting, it was not weird to me that people would grow food and raise chickens in their backyard. I was able to appreciate and understand the value of using any land you have, if you have the privilege of owning or having access to fertile land, to grow food.

SR: Please tell us a bit about the demographics of who took part in Occupy the Farm (OTF). I am particularly curious as to their relationship to food and to the community prior to their involvement. Were these farmers? Consumers? Activists? Environmentalists? Local residents? All of the above?

GO: *I was not very involved in the very first year, during the first big occupation, since I was doing an exchange program that year at UCLA. However, some of the key organizers, even before the first occupation, had reached out to me for help in strategizing because of my experience and connections with the MST. In fact, during that first occupation, the MST made a statement of solidarity with Occupy the Farm, prearranged by us. At that time, the movement was more about social justice more broadly than food justice specifically, since it was coming from the broader*

Occupy Movement in the Bay Area.

That was how I got involved, and those who brought me in also saw OTF as a way to take that vibrant political energy of the Occupy Movement from the urban centers out to the communities and neighborhoods. Occupy Wall Street had started in September of the year before (2011), and by October, there were tent cities in downtown squares like Oscar Grant plaza in Oakland, California and other places all over the country. The Occupy Movement was very different around the country, and my impression was that in most places it was a very white and middle-class protest movement: people would go out with signs to protest against the bail out of the banks, but there was very little radical action or deeper political struggle. In the Bay Area it was different, especially in Oakland, due to the longer history of class struggle, going back to early socialist labor unions through the Black Panthers, the ILWU (which is one of the most politicized labor unions in the country, shutting down the ports against the war in Iraq in 2003 for example), and more recently the struggles against gentrification and police brutality. That is why our occupation in downtown Oakland was named after Oscar Grant (who was murdered by the police a couple of years before). So, while the Occupy Movement was a relatively superficial protest movement in most places, it was different in the Bay Area. The tents in the occupation downtown were not just symbolic, like in many places. It was really about providing shelter to people who were homeless, it was about direct action to resolve our problems, rather than simply protesting against or in favor of some government policies. The occupation at Oscar Grant Plaza brought in shelter, food, resources, and a safe space for people who really needed it, and it gave visibility to the plight of people who were homeless and amplified their voice. Our movement soon grew to a general strike on November 2nd, which also shut down the port. We saw that as a direction for the movement to grow everywhere, and indeed on December 12th, there were port shutdowns along the entire west coast. Unfortunately, most other places did not radicalize like this. The movement continued to gain traction, but by late December and January, most occupations in major cities around the country— New York, LA, Chicago, etc.— had been disbanded. So there was a need to find constructive ways to sustain the movement after that.

Another important difference was that, while in many places there was something of a cult of "leaderlessness" and a dogmatic attitude that the movement was not about "making demands" (even if they were not in fact building [their] own solutions), the Occupy Movement in the Bay Area also grew from a very highly mobilized student movement that already had strong leadership and very clear demands preexisting the Occupy movement. After the budget cuts of 2008, leaders of the student movement launched massive occupations of buildings at Berkeley, successfully reversed some of the budget cuts, and later halted additional fee hikes. Communist, socialist, and anarchist graduate students took over our union, and we used it as a vehicle to channel resources to advance the struggle. For example, we hired buses to take students from the East Bay to downtown San Francisco where we occupied the Bank of America headquarters, combining the opposition against the banks who got bailed out with our struggle against the largest holder of student debt, and a Regent of the University of California also sits on the board of Bank of America, so we wanted to expose that conflict of interest. So, the strategy of occupations was already well-established in the Bay Area before the Occupy Wall Street mobilization in New York. And some of the key organizers in OTF came directly from these occupations by the student movement at Berkeley.

I would say, therefore, that it was a convergence of factors that created OTF. Many of the people who took part in Occupy the Farm did not come from the food movement and were just learning about agroecology, food justice, and food sovereignty on the spot. On the other hand, there were also a lot of people who were involved in the food movement for a much longer time, who came at it from various angles—environmental, health, spiritual—and who were then brought into the Occupy Movement and became radicalized into considering an approach (of land occupations) they may not have considered previously. Therefore, people outside of the food movement were brought into it, and people from the food movement were radicalized as a consequence of these mass mobilizations, which were themselves inspired in part by movements like MST.

SR: I see. So, you've just spoken a bit to this already, but I want to come back to this notion of context, the importance of setting. The writings of your colleague, Antonio Roman-Alcalá, strongly emphasize the fact that, when it comes to land struggles, context matters. The way land struggles play out in Northern settings, such as California, can be vastly different from how they do in Southern settings. You've already mentioned the national context, but can you speak a bit more to the ways in which you think Occupy the Farm was impacted by its local and regional contexts?

GO: *Well, for starters, before Occupy Wall Street, there had also been occupations of a lot of buildings on Berkeley campus. People from all over the Bay Area were involved, not just Berkeley students; and many of these people later joined the land occupation during Occupy the Farm. So, the number of participants we initially received, as well as the backgrounds of those participants, was certainly impacted by that.*

In most of the country, I think Occupy Wall Street was largely seen as a middle-class, white protest movement against the banks, and for a lot of them, the tents and the occupations were largely symbolic. However, in places like Oakland and many other parts of the country, gentrification and homelessness were already, and continued to be, a serious crisis. Because of this, the act of occupation and the use of tents were not just symbolic, but served the purposes of showing that there literally is a housing crisis and we need to create solutions for these displaced people.

That's what Occupy Oakland and Occupy the Farm did in the beginning— we created solutions for people in need, rather than just drawing attention to those needs. In the early days of both Occupy Oakland and Occupy the Farm, there were homeless people who would come to Occupy the Farm because they had been kicked out of Oscar Grant Plaza or other places. Not to romanticize the issue, but we were able to, in real time, provide a safe place with food and resources people needed. We didn't just make a symbolic gesture of solidarity.

An early question we asked ourselves during OTF was, "Can this be a movement of poor people? Can this be a movement about homelessness? Can this be a movement of the most marginalized?" However, that didn't really play out. The Gill Tract remained the focus right up to 2015, when we were able to secure the north side, but lost the south side and OTF largely demobilized. In all of those years (3-4 years) after the first mobilization, it had not become a movement of the most marginalized. There were strong contingents of students and political organizers— some of whom had stronger ties to the Food Movement and permaculture and so on, and some who did not; but the class character was not like movements such as MST, in the sense that it was not really a movement of poor people and for the poor. MST is largely a movement of actual landless people - the rural homeless. South Africa's Shack Dweller Movement— Abahlali baseMjondolo— is another example.

That kind of potential was there when things started, but, in part because of the context of people being middle class and not strictly hungry or strictly landless, it did not happen with OTF. There was this inability to organically integrate the homeless and make that part of the struggle.

SR: Guest editor of the Journal of Peasant Studies Raj Patel has written that egalitarianism is not so much a consequence of the politics of food sovereignty, but rather that it "is a prerequisite to have the democratic conversation about food policy in the first place." In other words, we cannot expect a truly democratic outcome in which control of land is directly in the hands of "the people" when those same people are oppressed by racism, sexism, classism, and so forth. With this in mind, given that we clearly do not have such an egalitarian society here in the U.S., to what extent can any food justice movement, or struggle for food sovereignty such as land occupation, be truly successful? Why are such efforts still worth undertaking even in an environment that is not conducive to them?

GO: *For me, it's about taking a dialectical approach to change, and recognizing that it might be three steps forward, one or two back, but we might still be able to make progress. That's just me being optimistic, perhaps, but… In the last year of OTF, we were just fighting for the south side (of the Gill Tract). The north was already the Gill Tract Community Farm. Many of the liberal Food Movement people who were, you know, less confrontational or less radicalized or whatever, they were verbally supportive still, but they did not actually go occupy. There was a clear North-vs.-*

South-side dynamic. In some ways, the victory of the north side created conditions to actually demobilize people for the struggle of the south side.

Within a year or so of the first occupation, we won a ten-year hold on the north side, but the south side was still slated for development. So, in the next couple of years, what was required was some of the, you know, "non-sexy" aspects of activism, like going to a lot of public meetings at the UC, town halls at Albany, collecting signatures, organizing a boycott campaign of Sprouts (the market that was proposing to build on the south side of the Gill Tract), and all of that, in an effort to halt development. When development was about to begin, there was an escalation. There were other attempts at occupation and other forms of disrupting construction. Unfortunately, those efforts failed.

The thing is, we knew at a certain point, to a certain extent, that we may be fighting a losing battle—that we were not going to get the south side, but we still valued the experience of direct action and organizing more radical tactics than were the norm at that time. We saw new generations of students and community members still coming to the movement, still attracted by the history of OTF, and we thought, "Look, we might not get the south side; but if we can share some of this knowledge, experience, and training we have of direct action with another generation, that would be really worthwhile." So, the educational aspect was pretty conscious for some of us. People might criticize that as paternalistic or a waste of people's time and energies and so on and so forth— and, by the way, that also reinforces the characteristic of the movement as being sort of cadre-led, as opposed to romanticized bottom-up organizing—but I just bite the bullet and say, "Yes, we need leadership. We need to learn from elders. We need to share experiences and training." I believe there is a lot of benefit to sharing these skills and this kind of politics, especially in moments of demobilization.

It is also important to note that 2015 was not the same context as 2011 or early 2012. It was not the moment when people were rushing to occupy something, and we were sucking out the air from some other struggle. We were, or at least we saw ourselves as, creating the conditions for radicalization that had retreated in the years since 2011 and early 2012. Maybe, in the future, if someone was inspired or galvanized by Occupy the Farm, if they participated and continue to have a political life, who is not to say that it was not a worthwhile struggle? Just because OTF did not grow into a poor peoples' movement, I certainly would not say that it reinforced the class and racial differences that really affect the food movement in the US, like the class privilege and white privilege we see around the consumer-oriented aspects of the movement. If anything, our continuation of radical action after the peak moment of the Occupy Movement, and growing connections with the MST in Brazil and other radical movements in the US and abroad, served to inject a more radical politics into privileged spaces of the food movement, across privileged neighborhoods in the Bay Area and broader permaculture and other events around California.

I see the question of egalitarianism and land struggle as a chicken-or-the-egg sort of argument. Multi-generational, multi-ethnic, multi-everything movements are fundamental so that we can continue to progress and not fall back so much, so that we can continue to make gains in the long term.

SR: Aside from holding the space, I understand that planting and harvesting took place during OTF— first planting during the initial occupation and then returning several times, at risk of arrest, to harvest food that was later distributed to the community. What did the day-to-day orchestration

of this look like? How did you manage to harvest so much food under such time-sensitive and labor-intensive conditions?

GO: *Well, unfortunately, I may not be the best person to ask because the most planting and harvesting took place during the very first occupation and I was not there for that. I was in LA working in media communications and relations with faculty at Berkeley and with the MST abroad, which is what I could do from afar. There were four or five occupations after that one, and except for one, they all involved planting. (One was led not by OTF but by the Indigenous Land Access Committee, and it was more ceremonial in nature. OTF participated, but we did not plant, and we left when the Indigenous Land Access Committee decided to leave.) However, we never planted as much as during that first time, and, as time wore on, we had more and more confrontations with the university as well as the police. We were learning about how they operated, and they were learning about how we operated. One of the things they learned is that even if they kicked us off the land, we could still send people back to hop the fence, water the plants, gather crops, and bring them over the fence for distribution. The university and police learned from their mistakes and became aware that if they wanted us to stop coming back to the land, just making us disperse was not going to be able to demobilize the movement as much. So, they started literally plowing under as much as possible as often as possible (by the 2nd or 3rd occupation, for sure). This not only ruined viable crops but also created problems with donations and participation, because people learned that this was happening and, if you collect a donation for 1,000 or so seedlings and then, they are all destroyed, people are less willing to donate to you again and participate in that planting.*

SR: I am familiar with the negative media campaign the university set in motion to discredit the

OTF movement, and I have often wondered about the extent to which there was direct communication between OTF and the university once the movement was underway. After an official appeal to the university was denied and development plans were made, how often, if at all, did OTF representatives appeal directly to the university to change course? Did anyone directly challenge the university regarding the falsehoods and misrepresentations it put out to discredit you, and, if so, how did the university attempt to justify this?

GO: *There was always an effort, on our part, to shift the topic of conversation— to not just respond to their accusations or to their narrative, but to try to change or control the narrative.*

A big challenge was that, when there wasn't a big, high-profile occupation going on, a lot of the local media didn't have interest in the story. So, part of the challenge was just getting attention. With respect to the university press, for example, the Daily Californian, some of the students were sympathetic or at least willing to do pretty good work with us, but a lot of them, not so much. There was pretty significant turn-around, and we often had to do a lot of "catch up" work with new student journalists so they could learn the narrative of our struggle and see through the narrative of the university.

The university would use the artificially-created housing crisis and used words like "develop" to make it sound like they were acting in the interests of the community. They even said they would put affordable housing on the land at some point. In return, we would say that we were researching agroecology, which was supposed to be the university's mission. Since it is a land grant institution, they are required by law to train the next generation of farmers and find solutions that benefit the community. The research that was happening there on integrated pest management (organic pest control as opposed to pesticides), for example, benefitted the community in the long-run in terms of environmental and public health. It also benefitted farmers by reducing their production costs, reducing their own exposure to carcinogenic pesticides, and so forth. However, there was a corporate capture of that mission - a corporate capture of the use of that land. Once they defunded the agroecology program to put biotech research facilities there, the biotech people didn't have a need for the land on the Gill Tract. You can read more about that in Bruce Jenning's article about this topic ("The killing fields: Science and politics at Berkeley, California, USA." Agriculture and Human Values 14: 259–271, 1997). At this point, we tried to shift the narrative to say, "Look, the amount of money you say the university will get privatizing and paving over this farm is nothing compared to the social benefit that agroecology research on this land can bring!" Estimates by Berkeley's own faculty in Environmental Science, Policy, and Management suggested the benefit to the state of California alone would run into the tens of millions of dollars from reduced pesticide use alone.

One other thing we tried, but was difficult to get the traction that we wanted, was to show that, at the same time that Berkeley was dismantling the Gill Tract, Stanford was building the O'Donohue Family Farm, which is named that because they were able to say, "Hey, we're Stanford! We're in California! Food sustainability is a hot topic here! Hey, O'Donohues, why don't you give us money to start an organic farm?!" And guess what? They did! They then started having tours and educational programs for middle-school and high-school students. And guess what? That also generated revenue! So, we tried to say, "Look, the money you're going to gain by developing this land is PEANUTS compared to both the societal, long-term benefits of what it is already being used for, and even the immediate, financial returns this can generate if you would just embrace, rather than resist, the idea of an agroecological community farm!"

This message was exceptionally hard for us to get out, though, because not only did we have trouble getting attention in general, but also, when we did, the media just wanted the "action shots," and they wanted to know things like, "How many people got arrested?", and what was our "sound bite". It was sad that we even needed those things to happen to get attention, and then when we did get some attention, that was all they wanted to talk about. We were always struggling to deepen the conversation.

SR: I know that many members of the Bay Area branch of Food Not Bombs were supportive of OTF, and the group has faced similar struggles regarding its use of People's Park. I wonder how familiar you are with that struggle, and whether you have any advice to offer about it?

GO: *Yes, there was lots of overlap amongst participants in these struggles, as well as the Albany Bulb— that's right on the waterfront in Albany, where there was a community of transient people who would camp out there, and they were displaced in 2013. There was not as strong or fruitful a connection as we would have wished, though, between these struggles, and I think this is in part because none of them really had the picture of a mass movement in mind. When you look at the (Global) South, again, the number of people involved is just so large, and people take on national-level banners of struggle and organize themselves into nation-wide mass movements. So, while all of these (OTF, Food not Bombs, resistance against eviction at the Albany Bulb, etc.) have clear similarities and interconnections, they still lack an overarching banner and an overarching structure of movement organization* *that I think could have translated those similarities into more effective coordination. This is something I am somewhat critical about.*

I am somewhat old-fashioned in the sense that I think we do need organizations, labor unions, working-class parties and such. We don't need to have an institutional and bureaucratic form necessarily, but we do need an organizational form. Food Not Bombs is exciting to me in that it is national, and also, to an extent, international, and it is also somewhat organizational—even though the chapters operate completely autonomously. So, when I talk about organization, I'm not really talking about bureaucracy, which is sometimes the criticism I get back when I start talking about this. There can be an overarching, organizational structure that isn't bureaucratic or cumbersome.

SR: I am also curious as to what you consider the extent of UC Berkeley's responsibility to its surrounding community (or that of any university, for that matter), and whether you feel, given the only partial success of OTF, as well as the continuing threat posed to People's Park, UC Berkeley is living up to this responsibility?

GO: *This conversation is usually about UC Berkeley's direct management of property in the East Bay. The thing is, the University of California is supposed to be a public institution, so it's not just about the local community of Berkeley to whom it is responsible; one must also ask, "What is the public mission of the university?" And this goes beyond its decision-making process about these plots of land. This goes down to the struggle over, even the research and the academic mission of, the university. So, why is it that the Gill Tract was no longer valued as farmland? Because they began to have research funded by and for the chemical* *and biotech industry, instead of agroecology. They defunded and dismantled the agroecology programs. Is the mission of the UC to do research that benefits the public, such as environmentally-sound pest management, which would help the people of California, farmers and consumers alike? But again, the university was not valuing this kind of research— agroecological research specifically—and that was a fundamental cause of its decision to "develop" the Gill Tract.*

SR: Please tell us what you are currently working on. I understand your focus has shifted in recent years to a more environmental lens. Can you elaborate about that?

GO: *My research at UC Berkeley was about the political ecology of agroindustrialization, and Chinese investments in Brazilian agribusiness, a research topic that I developed in collaboration with the MST, the Pastoral Commission on the Land (CPT) of the Catholic Church in Brazil, and other movements in La Via Campesina. I am continuing to develop that work now with a postdoctoral fellowship in environmental studies at Swarthmore College, and I continue to collaborate with social movements in the (Global) North and the (Global) South in these struggles. For example, since I found that the fear of a big "Chinese land grab" in Brazil was unsubstantiated, as the major land grabbers continue to be from the (Global) North, my research focus also shifted to the new financial instruments through which capital from the Global North is being channeled into land grabbing in Brazil, for example through the academic pension fund TIAA-CREF. This work is very much in collaboration with NGOs in the (Global) North and social movements in Brazil. My work on the role of Chinese capital has also shifted to their investments in infrastructure for South American integration, which is where that flow is much stronger and more strategic. I am also launching new* *research on the co-production of racial and environmental discourses about Asian migrations to South America. Much of this work continues in articulation with social movements in Brazil and abroad, including through the BRICS Initiative for Critical Agrarian Studies that I co-organize with several colleagues from around the world. My teaching at Swarthmore has also focused on agroecology and food sovereignty, and my current students, who are seniors in environmental studies, are co-developing grounded agroecological initiatives right here in Swarthmore itself. I have also maintained collaborations with networks of Brazilians and in solidarity with Brazilian social movements, especially as we tried to resist the parliamentary coup that deposed president Dilma Rousseff and her Workers' Party administration, and now resist the imposition of neoliberal policies, rolling back labor rights and environmental regulations, and aggravating human rights violations in Brazil.*

SR: Do you see any overlap between your current work and the issues that lead to the necessity for land movements such as Occupy the Farm? Has your current work impacted the way you view these movements?

GO: *Absolutely. The United States is poised to face another major economic crisis like the one from 2007 to 2009, and the issues at the heart of the food movement, and the need for that radicalization that emerged with the Occupy Movement are very much still pertinent today. In fact, my sense is that these initiatives that create convergences like OTF, bringing together people from cultural milieus like the food movement, and more radical organizers who have experience and dedication to advance the struggle, are needed even more now in the (Global) North and the (Global) South alike. I see, for example, how our movements in the US in solidarity with the Left in Brazil were very weak, unable to* *contribute much in face of the right-wing parliamentary coup in Brazil – and perhaps if we had several groups like OTF thriving in the US that could have served as a platform for stronger solidarity.*

Regarding movements within the US itself, the latest presidential election has given me an even greater sense of how important that conjuncture of factors was in the Bay Area at that moment and how much class struggle and strong organizations are needed in face of the right-wing advancements we see in the US right now. This is something that goes directly against the way that "identity politics" has become the fulcrum of political organizing (both in the Left and the Right) in the US. Without a strong sense of class as the basis for our struggle, and without strong class-based organizations, our struggles become reduced to separate, "unrelated movements with specific purposes", with no common ground except for a toothless support for the Democratic Party's decaying strategy to sustain neoliberalism at all cost– to the point of sabotaging a social-democratic campaign with mass support just in order to maintain elite control of the party, even at the cost of losing the presidential election. And of course, it is "identity politics" that mobilizes the white working class into conservative, nationalist, even fascist movements, ultimately rallying behind the corporate elite against their own class interest.

What is currently lacking among leftist social movements in the US (after the Occupy Movement) is a grounded sense of class struggle, which is a struggle for territory, a struggle for popular sovereignty, which becomes a struggle for food sovereignty when articulated with the food movement.

Nonetheless, as I explained before about holding a dialectical view of social change, I am confident that our current work struggling for land redistribution, agrarian reform, and revolutionary social transformation all around the world can make progress as we continue to learn from our experiences, at home and abroad, to liberate the commons and cultivate community.

Citations

1. *Declaration of the Forum for Food Sovereignty, Nyéléni.* Held in Nyéléni Village, Sélingué, Mali. February 27, 2007.

2. "Landless Workers' Movement." Wikipedia entry. Accessed June 18, 2018.

3. Roman-Alcalá, Antonio. "Broadening the Land Question in Food Sovereignty to Northern Settings: A Case Study of Occupy the Farm." *Globalizations*, Vol. 12, Issue 4: Food Sovereignty: Concept, Practice, and Social Movements. Pages 545-558. 2015.

4. "What is the MST?" MSTBrazil.Org. Accessed February 4, 2018.

5. Roman-Alcalá, Antonio. "Broadening the Land Question in Food Sovereignty to Northern Settings: A Case Study of Occupy the Farm." *Globalizations*, Vol. 12, Issue 4: Food Sovereignty: Concept, Practice, and Social Movements. Pages 545-558. 2015.

6. "Landless Workers' Movement." Wikipedia entry. Accessed June 18, 2018.

7. Ibid.

8. Roman-Alcalá, Antonio. "Broadening the Land Question in Food Sovereignty to
Northern Settings: A Case Study of Occupy the Farm." *Globalizations*, Vol. 12, Issue 4: Food Sovereignty:

Concept, Practice, and Social Movements. Pages 545-558. 2015.

9. Ibid.

10. Roman-Alcalá, Antonio. "Occupy the Farm: A Study of Civil Society Tactics to Cultivate Commons and Construct Food Sovereignty in the United States." *The Journal of Peasant Studies*, published by Yale University's Program in Agrarian Studies. From Food Sovereignty: A Critical Dialogue International Conference at Yale, September 14-15, 2013.

11. La Via Campesina Organizational Brochure, 2016 Edition. Excerpt published October 28, 2016.

12. Roman-Alcalá, Antonio. "Occupy the Farm: A Study of Civil Society Tactics to Cultivate Commons and Construct Food Sovereignty in the United States." *The Journal of Peasant Studies*, published by Yale University's Program in Agrarian Studies. From Food Sovereignty: A Critical Dialogue International Conference at Yale, September 14-15, 2013.

13. Patel, Raj. "Food Sovereignty." *The Journal of Peasant Studies*, Volume 36, Issue 3. 2009. Pages 663-706.

14. Jennings, Bruce H. "The killing fields: Science and politics at Berkeley, California, USA." *Journal of Agriculture*

and Human Values, Volume 14. The Netherlands: Kluwer Academic Publishers, 1997. Pages 259-271.

15. Ibid.

16. Ibid.

17. Van den Bosch, Robert. *The Pesticide Conspiracy*. Garden City, New York: Doubleday, 1978.

18. Roman-Alcalá, Antonio. "Broadening the Land Question in Food Sovereignty to
Northern Settings: A Case Study of Occupy the Farm." *Globalizations*, Vol. 12, Issue 4: Food Sovereignty: Concept, Practice, and Social Movements. Pages 545-558. 2015.

19. Roman-Alcalá, Antonio. "Occupy the Farm: The Legitimacy of Direct Action to Create Land Commons." From *Land Justice: Re-imagining Land, Food, and the Commons in the United States*. Edited by Justine M. Williams and Eric Holt-Giménez. Oakland, California: Food First Books, 2017.

20. Ibid.

CHAPTER FIVE

Food Without Borders: Xenophobia and Global Corporatism in the U.S.-Mexico Agricultural Commerce

By Lilia Trenkova

According to a January 2016 Oxfam report, worldwide, "In 2015, just 62 individuals had the same wealth as 3.6 billion people—the bottom half of humanity."[1] Meanwhile, 1 in 9 humans on the planet lives in extreme poverty and hunger.[2] The post-World War II categories of first-, second- and third-world countries are just as divided and hierarchical as they were in the 1950s. Despite an increasingly globalized world economy, very few *developing* countries have *developed*[3] in accordance to the Western model. Instead of increasing the wealth of nations, globalization has increased the wealth of multinational corporations based in already-wealthy countries, such as the United States.[4] With agriculture now a global industry, and one increasingly profiting from animal bodies,[5] food production and access are intertwined with economic, environmental, labor and social justice more than ever. With the support of government subsidies and international legislation, the agriculture industry drives people worldwide to consume more animal bodies. As a result, this growing animal agriculture causes increasing harm to not only its nonhuman victims and the environment as a whole, but also its workforce, which is dependent predominantly on the labor of migrants—whether in developed or developing countries.

Neocolonialism and Economic "Development"

While so-called economic development is measured using a variety of factors (GDP, national income, per capita income growth, etc.), it provides no metrics for or control over wealth distribution. A country may qualify as *developed* while the majority of its citizens still struggle with stagnant wages and poverty. In a *developing* country, foreign investments rarely create local jobs with growth potential. Instead, they create an economic dependence, one that ultimately still benefits the *developed* country more than the *developing* (or *other*, *not-so-developed*) country.

This economic dependence has been aptly called *neocolonialism*. Like its predecessor, colonialism, neocolonialism involves acquisition of control. In the 1500-1900 colonial Americas, for instance, this control was directly over land and people governance; today, this neocolonial control is indirect, using the countries' economies and legislation to gain access to its land and people. Both colonialism and neocolonialism are founded on the xenophobic (and usually racist) premise that the *other* (country, nation, etc.) is *lesser than*, not equal to, one's own— a resource, rather than a partner. Both ultimately result in inequity and injustice, from basic human rights to food supply and government regulation.

Herein, I will focus on the United States and Mexico as an example of two countries with a long-shared social and economic history centered largely on food supply and trade, from pre-colonial times through periods of colonization, and into their current neocolonial relationship. Through this case study, I will track how colonizing practices and their nationalistic roots have led to the increasing wealth and food access disparity that prevails throughout Mexican populations in both countries. I will examine how agriculture, and in particular animal agriculture, has been the driving tool for colonial and capitalist control. In conclusion, I will argue that food justice movements should work not only towards decentralized and horizontal economic models for food supply, but also towards models in which animal agriculture no longer exists and in which plant *monoculture* (growing a single species over a large amount of land) farming is replaced by *polyculture* (growing many species) *agroecology* (agriculture that embodies ecological principles.)

Colonization and Agriculture in the United States

When it comes to agricultural labor, the United States has always had a dark history, from African slaves to migrants from countries like Mexico, China and the Philippines throughout the nineteenth and twentieth centuries.[6] Today, over two-thirds of farm workers in the U.S. originate from Mexico, and most of them are undocumented.[7, 8]

Only twice in U.S. history have farm workers been predominantly white citizens. The first time was in the beginning of the North American colonization, when English and German migrants would become "indentured servants" by exchanging years of their labor for travel costs and their right to live as a *citizen* of the colonies. Since the indenture was limited to a certain number of years, this meant that free labor, too, was time-sensitive. As colonies grew, the indenture practice became less profitable, so farm owners began using enslaved Africans for fieldwork.

The second time was during the Great Depression. During that period, many white farm- and business-owners sold their properties and became migrant farm workers, traveling to wherever they could find work. Just prior to the Depression, and since the 1833 Abolition of Slavery Act, farm workers had become increasingly and predominantly Mexican migrants. As the Depression resulted in fewer jobs to go around, the U.S. gave priority to its white citizen population. As a result, over half a million Mexicans were deported in the 1930s, an organized government effort euphemistically called the *Mexican Repatriation.*

Just a few years later, as there was a shortage of labor in the U.S. because of World War II, the U.S. government once again opened its borders to Mexican migrants looking for jobs on farms, this time through what was called the *bracero* program. The program did provide a legal, albeit temporary, status to migrant workers, but it did nothing to ensure fair wages, working conditions, and treatment. Today, the bracero program has been replaced by the H-2 visa guest worker program, which isn't any different in practice. From the bracero program through today, workers have been regularly cheated out of wages, placed in deplorable, overcrowded housing, forced to work long hours, and subjected to verbal and physical abuse by their higher-ups.[9] Workers in animal agriculture facilities have an added layer of emotional and psychological trauma as the very nature of their work is founded on systemic and mechanized killing.[10]

Colonization and Agriculture in Mexico

Mexico, too, has a nefarious agricultural past. Spanish colonizers in the 1500s imposed an essentially feudal system over indigenous people for the entire three centuries (1500s-1800s) of *Virreinato de Nueva España* (or "Viceroyalty of New Spain," the name they gave to their colony in mainland America, north of the Isthmus of Panama).[11] The Spanish were also the ones to introduce cows, pigs, chickens, and horses to the continent and surrounding islands, forever disrupting local ecologies and food traditions, as well as laying the bodies of these animals at the foundation of today's anti-indigenous, racist, and xenophobic food system.[12]

Even after Mexico gained its independence in 1821, this feudal system remained the same, but with a new form of governance which kept indigenous people at the disadvantaged end and gave the upper-class reign over land and labor. The nineteenth century in Mexico, especially during the Porfirio Diaz dictatorship, became a prime example of neocolonialism: foreign companies and individuals (mostly from the U.S., such as J. P. Morgan and the Guggenheims) purchased and controlled large amounts of land for agricultural production, oil, and mining. Rather than profiting the Mexican population, these foreign "investments" paid overworked locals poorly and collected their profits back into their respective countries.[13]

After the 1910 Mexican Revolution, there was a wave of radical reversal—most notably during the Lázaro Cárdenas presidency (1934-1940), when land previously owned by commercial landholders was distributed among the population, most large foreign trusts (such as those in oil) ceased, and industries nationalized. The ensuing years of *import-substitution* economy grew Mexico's industry but did not solve any of the issues of wealth disparity and poverty that the country faced. Furthermore, as Mexico industrialized, more and more state funds were put into developing urban industrial centers, and less and less state funding went into maintaining rural infrastructure or services, including education.

This pushed people from rural, agrarian areas to migrate either into urban, industrial ones or to the U.S. as farm workers, especially after the North American Free Trade Agreement (NAFTA) became active in 1994,[14] when foreign companies were incentivized to once again plant production roots in Mexico through the reduction of import tariffs.

NAFTA, Migration, and Xenophobia

It makes sense that the U.S. and Mexico are closely tied economically, albeit unfairly. The two are neighboring countries; the U.S. has more agricultural jobs than it has citizens who want to work in them, and Mexico has the opposite problem— more farm workers in need of jobs than positions for them. How did the U.S.'s surplus and Mexico's deficit in the agricultural job sector come to be?

Farm workers in Mexico already struggled before the passing of NAFTA. After the agreement, they were simply defeated. Corn farmers, for instance (who, in Mexico, do not receive any government subsidies) had to compete with a market now saturated with corn imported by large-scale U.S. producers (who *do* receive U.S. government subsidies).[15] NAFTA did not create nearly enough new jobs to absorb the unemployed farmers, so people were pushed to either poverty or migration (or both).[16,17] NAFTA is an economic embodiment of first-world xenophobia: taking advantage of citizens of *other* countries for cheap labor and high profits, while demonizing and violating the rights of these same individuals within one's own borders— basic rights such as those of food security.[18]

The jobs that NAFTA did create have been in the *maquiladora* sector: assembly factories close to the Mexico-U.S. border or near urban centers, owned by foreign corporations and employing hundreds of thousands of people at low wages, with no upward mobility. Such factories are allowed to import materials and equipment and export finished products free of tariffs, thus only contributing to Mexico as job providers— extremely low-paying job providers.

None have profited as much from NAFTA, however, as animal agribusiness giants like Smithfield Foods (largest farmer of pigs worldwide) and Cargill (one of the largest farmers of cows).[19] These top-down mega corporations followed the same model as the *maquiladoras* when setting up their own facilities, securing a double profit, both in Mexico and in the U.S. A sample profit cycle can include: growing corn in the U.S. for cheap (because of USDA subsidies), exporting that corn into Mexico for cheap to sell (essentially to themselves) as food for the pigs in their Mexico facility, and then selling the bodies of those pigs for cheap in both Mexico and back into the U.S., This, in a nutshell, is how NAFTA and U.S. Big Ag have killed Mexico's millennia-old corn farming tradition. Where corn has been a staple, locally-grown human food, it has now become an import fed not so much to humans but to pigs, who are in turn killed and fed to humans, profiting companies like Smithfield Foods.

Ironically, in the U.S., these corporations also employ Mexico's migrant farm workers— in both plant and animal agriculture so that they can get away with the same low-wage and union-suppression practices as they do in their Mexican counterparts.[20]

NAFTA and other similar agreements (such as the Trans-Pacific Partnership), which in theory serve to "free" the trade market, in fact empower already-powerful corporations to take over markets in *developing* countries freely and without obstruction. They claim to level the playing field, and yet the field can never be level when the players aren't even starting under the same conditions, much less have access to the same equipment.

Today's globalized economy isn't just a competition over market shares and resources. Countries like Mexico have an immense disadvantage to countries like the U.S. that runs deeper than negotiating skills and internal government corruption. It is a social disadvantage, founded on xenophobia: the discriminatory presumption that citizens of *other* (non-U.S.) countries are inferior and/or threatening to *our* (U.S.) citizens.

Historically, Mexican migrant laborers have only been brought into the U.S. when there has been a surplus of jobs that U.S. citizens are largely unwilling to do (in intensive and high-risk fields, such as agriculture). Both their employing corporations and the U.S. government regard this particular immigrant group as an economic unit, not as a social demographic with basic needs such as housing, education, family services and healthcare. Migrant laborers are dispensable and are subject to deportation at any moment: when their employer downsizes or relocates their operation,[21] when they demand equal rights,[22] or when Immigration and Customs Enforcement (ICE) conducts a mass raid.[23] "The current enforcement policy is based on excluding [migrants], through violence and jail at the border, and isolation and fear in their community. The idea is to make life so hard for them in the US they'll have to leave," says Rivera Salgado, a Mixteco professor at UCLA.[24]

The demonization in the U.S. of Mexican immigrants, meanwhile, is evidenced by portrayals of Mexicans in mainstream U.S. media as "illegal" or "uneducated."[25] Racist and xenophobic stereotyping is so rampant that it even shows in the rhetoric of major political leaders. Notable examples appear in speeches by Donald Trump, in which he has used xenophobia as a prop for his presidential platform. He has said that, "When Mexico sends its people, they're not sending their best. They're sending people that have lots of problems, and they're bringing those problems with us. They're bringing drugs. They're bringing crime. They're rapists. And some, I assume, are good people." His solution to this alleged problem? "We're going to do a wall; we're going to have a big, fat beautiful door on the wall; we're going to have people come in, but they're going to come in legally. [...] Mexico's going to pay for the wall."[26]

In addition, Trump condemns NAFTA for having destroyed the U.S. auto industry and taken jobs overseas while ignoring the plight of Mexican farmers resulting from NAFTA. One could ascribe his views to xenophobia: he cherry-picks NAFTA's detriments and only points out the ones that invoke nationalist nostalgia for an industry that has long been a symbol of the U.S. economy as a way to attract support from the U.S. citizen working class and further distance them from the immigrant working class.

Within Mexico, the *maquiladora* industry brings high profits to corporations but not to the Mexican citizens who work in the sector—again because of the xenophobic position that employees in *other* countries are inferior and therefore deserving of less financial reward and quality of work conditions than *our* employees.

Xenophobic corporate practices are one of the many offenses of the oligarchic capitalist system that reigns over most of the world today. Governments have not only failed to regulate corporations; they have also been directly complicit in concentrating power and wealth into the bank accounts of the already wealthy.[27]

In the U.S., the government has also failed to recognize the basic rights of its noncitizen constituents (documented or undocumented) and continuously discriminates against immigrants and their needs through its public assistance programs. Unlike their citizen counterparts, poor and low-income undocumented immigrants in the U.S. are not eligible for any of the significant benefit programs such as Medicaid or SNAP (Supplemental Nutrition Assistance Program)[28] despite the fact that they contribute over $11 billion in state and local taxes per year by merely existing and paying sales tax on basic items, like food and clothing, or property tax on housing.[29] (Those who use false social security numbers also end up paying income tax, though they will never see any retirement benefits in the future.)

Public assistance is inaccessible even for some poor and low-income *documented* immigrants. People with a temporary residence status, for instance, are just as ineligible as those who are undocumented, and even those who gain *legal* permanent residency need to wait five years in order to begin to receive benefits.[30]

The combination of forced migration and lack of public access to basic resources drives a large number of immigrants in the U.S., documented or undocumented, into working in agriculture. Agriculture, as described earlier, has formed a symbiotic relationship with the xenophobic corporatist government: a bond so strong that it will take a great deal of effort to free people from its grip.

Going Forward: Advocacy and Solutions

To counter the damaging effects of centralized and globalized markets, communities across the world are creating cooperatives, small-scale polyculture farms and worker-owned businesses. There are about 30,000 worker cooperatives in the U.S.,[31] and their numbers continue to rise with the help of incubator programs like the Worker Co-op Academy and Prospera in the San Francisco Bay Area, as well as the success of community initiatives, such as Equal Exchange in Boston.

The Worker Co-op Academy is a collaborative project

by multiple Bay Area nonprofit organizations that assists low- and moderate-income community members in starting worker-owned businesses for and in their own communities. Prospera helps another specific demographic, Latina women, to do the same. Equal Exchange has taken the cooperative vision international, and has created a commerce network for fairly traded products such as coffee and cocoa between farmer co-ops in the Americas, Asia and Africa, and buyers in the U.S.

In Southern Mexico, the Zapatista communities are using agroecology as one of the many tools for organizing social autonomy. Reclaiming the indigenous traditions of polyculture farming (planting multiple species together; opposite of monoculture) and growing native plants such as corn, beans and squash together (a combination known as the "three sisters"), food production becomes an act of resistance and regeneration at the same time. Resistance to the multibillion dollar animal agriculture industries that grab and destroy land, habitat, and plant-based food traditions—and as a result a regeneration of that same land, habitat, and plant-based food traditions.[32] The very nature of monoculture is in fact xenophobic: homogeneity is the goal, and any other plant species is viewed as a "threat" or an "invader". Polyculture, on the other hand, embraces species diversity, which in turn causes all participating species to thrive as they support one another.

Polyculture farming can also include so-called "cash crops," or higher-value crops for market. For example, Zapatista farmers have been able to receive income from outside their community by growing and selling coffee. Fair-trade organic coffee cooperatives overall have grown significantly over the last two decades, due to an increase in buyer interest from the U.S. and Europe (i.e. places where people can afford to pay more), contributing to higher income for farmers and their families. Higher income means better access to food and housing, as well as a weaker push factor that drives so many people to migrate north or to the U.S. in search of jobs. Better wages and the ability to stay put, in turn, result in parents being able to invest in their children's education.[33] Fair business practices and transactions result in parties treating one another as equals, regardless of origin country or citizenship status.

Small-scale, worker-owned farms and networks like the veganic Grow Where You Are farm in Atlanta, GA, provide support to like-minded growers and build collective resilience to mainstream agriculture. The collective provides education and trainings in agroecology and urban farm development while also demonstrating a sustainable business model that brings in high value for their crops through a community supported agriculture (CSA) subscription-based distribution.

At the grassroots activism and community organizing level, the Food Empowerment Project has been the first organization to envision and incite a food justice movement that extends its liberation goals across species lines. From offering an ever-evolving database of fair-trade chocolate producers, to fighting for legislation protecting farm workers, to protesting animal farms that harm nonhumans and humans, the Food Empowerment Project demonstrates that it is in fact possible to advocate for multiple forms of justice at once, and that the liberation of animals is very much a food justice issue (and vice versa).

It is important to note that all of these initiatives and

organizations are impactful and empowering precisely *because* they tackle multiple issues at once. They embody the means towards a collective end: a beginning phase of longer-term power reclamation and the creation of a new system—one that benefits the many, not the few. Single-purpose community gardens and farmers' markets, for instance, will never measure up without being grounded in justice; in fact, in some instances, they can even have a negative effect on a community, as is the case in many gentrifying neighborhoods throughout the U.S.[34]

These initiatives should always be parts of larger movements that include and empower underprivileged communities (people of color, immigrants—documented or undocumented, low-income families, women, queer people, and, yes, nonhuman animals). The Zapatistas do precisely this by enabling not only its own members, but also the extended community to live better through education, as well as the products from their farms; their goals aren't limited to satisfying their own needs. Grow Where You Are does this too, by providing support and educational resources to next-generation farmers while also feeding their local communities healthy, local, fair-labor produce, without the use of any animal "inputs".

Equal Exchange follows the same principles by working *with*, not above, farmers— in complete contrast with many U.S. companies, like Smithfield Foods. Smithfield Foods adopts the colonialist extractive and xenophobic approach with its facilities in Mexico:[35] animals are objects, workers are disposable, and all that matters is the profit gained by the company. Equal Exchange, on the other hand, adopts a sustainable and inclusive model centered around profit *sharing*.

Conclusion

The U.S.-Mexico relationship is a classic example of free-market neocolonialism. The xenophobic presumption that one nation is above another and may oppress people from another country so as to neutralize an unspoken *threat* they are believed to pose, results in a dynamic in which the more powerful of the two can dictate the rules and leave the weaker to fend for itself— or, in the case of Mexico and its traditionally corrupt government, to fend for its elite.

The ever-globalizing free-market capitalism in place today will continue to cause food access disparity as long as it continues to perpetuate social discrimination (such as xenophobia, classism, and nationalism); increased animal commodification will only add an exponential factor towards worsening the inequalities. Initiatives that strive to offset the imbalance will only succeed if they address the bigger picture and work at solving the problem with not only a national but also an *inter*national impact. On the local and national level, these should include community-owned land and businesses, such as Grow Where You Are and the Zapatista cooperatives. On the global level, these should include horizontally structured multinational networks, like Equal Exchange. We also need an even stronger food justice movement that addresses the needs of and empowers farm workers through efforts firmly grounded in total liberation for humans and nonhumans. We can already witness the immense impact of such a stance through the work the Food Empowerment Project spearheads.

Colonialist capitalism is a complex system, so we need to attack it on all fronts in order to dismantle it. From grassroots advocacy to how we run our businesses, we each can— and should— play our part, together in solidarity, always holding and uplifting those who need it more than we do.

Citations

1. "An Economy for the 1%: How Privilege and Power in the Economy Drive Extreme Inequality and How This Can Be Stopped." Rep. Oxfam, January 18, 2016.

2. "The State of Food Insecurity in the World." Rep. FAO, 2015.

3. "Country Classification." Rep. UN, 2014.

4. Woellert, Lorraine. "Corporate 1% in U.S. Gets Wealthier While Cash Piles Up." *Bloomberg*. August 8, 2014.

5. Bruinsma, Jelle, editor. "Livestock Production." *World Agriculture: Towards 2015/2030: an FAO Perspective*. Earthscan, 2003, pp. 162–163.

6. "Timeline of Agricultural Labor in the U.S." Rep. Youth & Young Adult Network of the National Farm Worker Ministry, November 2011.

7. "Facts about Farm Workers." Rep. National Center for Farmworker Health, Inc., August 2012.

8. "Migrant and Seasonal Farmworker Demographics Fact Sheet." Rep. National Center for Farmworker Health, Inc., September 2012.

9. Bauer, Mary, and Meredith Stewart. "Close to Slavery: Guestworker Programs in the United States." Rep. The Southern Poverty Law Center, February 18, 2013.

10. Dillard, Jennifer, A Slaughterhouse Nightmare: Psychological Harm Suffered by Slaughterhouse Employees and the Possibility of Redress through Legal Reform. Georgetown Journal on Poverty Law & Policy, 2008.

11. "Viceroyalty of New Spain." Encyclopædia Britannica, Encyclopædia Britannica, Inc., 31 May 2013.

12. Alvarez, Linda. "Colonization, Food, and the Practice of Eating." Food Empowerment Project.

13. De Regil, Alvaro J. "The Case of Mexico I: Neo-Colonialism and Truncated Revolution." *The Neo-Capitalist Assault*, 2001.

14. De Regil, Alvaro J. "The Case of Mexico II: Globalization and Destitution." *The Neo-Capitalist Assault*, 2001.

15. Zepeda, Eduardo, Wise, Timothy A. and Gallagher, Kevin P. "Rethinking Trade Policy for Development: Lessons from Mexico Under NAFTA." Rep. Carnegie Endowment for International Peace, December 2009.

16. González, Eduardo, Jr. "Migrant Farm Workers: Our Nation's Invisible Population." October 5, 2015.

17. Bacon, David. "Globalization and NAFTA Caused Migration from Mexico." *The Public Eye*, Fall 2014. Political Research Associates, October 11, 2014.

18. Carlsen, Laura. "NAFTA Is Starving Mexico Free Trade Has Starved Mexico and Stuffed Transnational Corporations." *Foreign Policy in Focus,* October 20, 2011.

19. Spieldoch, Alexandra. "NAFTA: Fueling Market Concentration in Agriculture." Institute for Agriculture and Trade Policy, 2010.

20. Bacon, David. *The Right to Stay Home: How U.S. Policy Drives Mexican Migration*. Boston: Beacon, 2013.

21. Barnes, Kathryn. "Mass Layoffs Hit Undocumented Farmworkers in Santa Maria." *For the Curious*. KCRW, March 25, 2016.

22. "Dreamer Activist Deported after Protesting US Immigration Policy." *RT*, October 30, 2013.

23. Hsu, Spencer S. "Immigration Raid Jars a Small Town." *Washington Post*. May 18, 2008.

24. Bacon, David. "Oaxaca's "Occupier" Refugees Face Roadblocks on the Way Home." *Truthout*, January 30, 2012.

25. *The Impact of Media Stereotypes on Opinions and Attitudes Towards Latinos*. Rep. National Hispanic Media Coalition, September 2012.

26. Imbert, Fred. "Donald Trump: Mexico Going to Pay for Wall." Republican Presidential Debate, broadcast on CNBC. October 28, 2015.

27. *Five Years after Market Crash, U.S. Economy Seen as 'No More Secure'*. Rep. Pew Research Center, September 12, 2013.

28. Ku, Leighton, and Brian Bruen. *Poor Immigrants Use*

Public Benefits at a Lower Rate than Poor Native-Born Citizens. Publication. Cato Institute Center for Global Liberty and Prosperity, March 4, 2013. Web.

29. Gee, Lisa Christensen, Matthew Gardner, and Meg Wiehe. *Undocumented Immigrants' State & Local Tax Contributions.* Publication. The Institute on Taxation & Economic Policy, February 2016.

30. Peña, Devon G., and Gallo Téenek. "Autonomy More than Direct Democracy: Indigenous Farming, Foods and Foodways Are Core Values." *Environmental and Food Justice*, 14 Mar. 2014.

31. *Research on the Economic Impact of Cooperatives.* Rep. University of Wisconsin Center for Cooperatives.

32. Peña, Devon G., and Gallo Téenek. "Autonomy More than Direct Democracy: Indigenous Farming, Foods and Foodways Are Core Values." *Environmental and Food Justice*, 14 Mar. 2014.

33. Gitter, Seth A., Jeremy G. Weber, Bradford I. Barham, Mercedes Callenes, and Jessa Lewis Valentine. "Fair Trade-Organic Coffee Cooperatives, Migration, and Secondary Schooling in Southern Mexico." *Journal of Development Studies* 48.3 (n.d.): 445-63. Routlege, Taylor & Francis Group, March 2012.

34. Newkirk, Vann R., II. "Irrigating the (Food) Desert: A Tale of Gentrification in D.C." Web log post. *Gawker.* N.p., 11 August 2014.

35. Carlsen, Laura. "NAFTA Is Starving Mexico: Free

trade has starved Mexico and stuffed transnational corporations." *Foreign Policy in Focus*, February 20, 2011.

CHAPTER SIX

Food Justice and Race in the U.S.

By Starr Carrington

The phenomenon of food swamps is a huge threat to the decolonization of Black people's diets, as it maintains a food environment that leads people of color, in a state of hopelessness, to entirely preventable deaths. To analyze this threat within a social context, one must consider the differences between food deserts and food swamps, as well as what these food environments look like and how they affect populations across the U.S. This is the first step in identifying the roles and impact of race on food justice, food access, and food awareness. In doing so, we may be called to question the ways in which our knowledge of food habits and consumer choices is influenced by deeply-ingrained societal factors rather than superficial, individual choice.

Food Deserts vs. Food Swamps

Food access in predominantly-white, middle-income areas, on average, far exceeds food access to predominantly Black, low-income areas, which represents a racial divide within our food system. While this may be common knowledge, the root of this social issue is seldom addressed within a global context. Too often, this issue is regarded on a level of individual behavior, which is often a debilitating approach to public health issues.

According to the Food Access Research Atlas published by United States Department of Agriculture,[1] *food deserts* are defined as neighborhoods and communities that are devoid of fresh produce and healthful, whole foods. Clear indicators of a food desert are an eminent lack of grocery stores, farmers' markets, and healthy food providers. A common way to identify a food desert is by calculating not only one's distance from the nearest grocery store, but also by evaluating the level of poverty and access to transportation within this neighborhood or community. The median household income within a typical food desert is less than 185 percent of the federal poverty level for a family of four, and over 40 percent of residents thereof do not have access to a vehicle.[2]

Johns Hopkins Center for a Livable Future defines a *food swamp* as a food environment *within* a food desert where unhealthy food is more readily available than healthy foods. So, while this particular area may lack fresh produce and healthful whole foods, it is simultaneously abundant in unhealthful fast food options.

Predominantly Black zip codes have fewer than half

the number of chain supermarkets in comparison to predominantly white zip codes.[3] For example, in the suburb of Fairfax County, Virginia, just about 10 to 30 miles outside of the city, access to quality produce and vegan alternatives is quite high. In Fairfax County, only 10.2 percent of residents identified as Black or African-American alone and 16.1 percent of residents identified as Hispanic or Latino on the 2016 census.[4] As 65.8 percent of residents identify as White alone, this is definitely a predominantly white area. Both Wards 7 and 8 of the District of Columbia, by contrast, have a population that is 93 percent Black or African-American alone.

As of 2014, there is an estimated total of 189 grocery stores per 1.1 million residents within Fairfax County. Out of this large number, residents have access to at least three Whole Foods Market locations, all of which contain several plant-based options, meat alternatives, dairy/egg substitutes, as well as healthful, high-quality produce sold at notoriously high prices. In this food environment, the average number of grocery stores per 150,000 residents would be 30.

A 2017 report by D.C. Hunger Solutions displayed that Wards 7 and 8 of D.C. had only three grocery stores for just under 150,000 residents.[5] The mostly-white town of Herndon, just 35 miles away from Ward 7, has *twice* the number of grocery stores for its just under 25,000 residents.

More than three quarters of all food deserts in D.C. are located within Wards 7 and 8. Consequently, these wards yielded D.C.'s highest rate of obesity and diabetes in 2012, with numbers exceeding the city's overall averages.

From the evidence provided, we can conclude that there is a food access gap that has a negative impact on the health of Black people, particularly in the D.C. Metropolitan Area.

The Impacts of Food Swamps

The top three leading causes of death for the Black and Latinx populations in the United States are heart disease, cancer and stroke.[6] According to the CDC, 57 percent of Black women and 38 percent of Black men aged 20 and over in the United States experience obesity. The same is true for 45 percent of Latinx women and 39.7 percent of Latinx men aged 20 and over.[7] These numbers may not seem concerning, considering the overall state of our health as a nation— until compared to the obesity rates of non-Hispanic White men and women aged 20 and over. Only 35 percent of this population of men and women *combined* experience obesity. A study by Rudd Center for Food Policy and Obesity found that simply residing within a food swamp, a factor often out of one's control, is an increasingly relevant predictor of obesity— even more so than living in a food desert. The data reflects the fact that food swamps are heavily populated by Black and/or Latinx impoverished communities. In concurrence, Black and Latinx populations currently have the highest rates of childhood obesity.[8]

Furthermore, food consumption and regulation has been used by white men as a method of displaying ownership over bodies of color. Within the dynamic from which traditional soul food originated, the "master" controlled when, where, what, and how an enslaved Black person was fed. In this food system, through direct physical means, an outside entity has control over one's food choices, food access, and food quality. In a modern society, fast food and low-quality produce represent the scraps of the food industry.

Naa Oyo A. Kwate, PhD at the Center for Race and Ethnicity at Rutgers University evaluated the sociological consequences of the shared geographic location of Black people and fast food.[9] Dr. Kwate highlighted the toxic association of Black people with fast food consumption as well as health-related conditions. Without cultural context and critical analysis, the narrative suggests that the "polluted" Black population deserves to experience these health outcomes because its health experience is a result of individual dietary choices, overwhelming gluttony, and general carelessness about one's health.

Through environmental racism, fast food is delegated to communities of color at disproportionate rates.

The fast food industry makes profit from exploiting people experiencing poverty by forcing them to consuming the scraps of the food industry. I compare fast food to scraps because the meat given to large chain fast food restaurants is often from dairy cows who experienced disease or extreme fatigue from exploitation. Essentially, this is what cannot be sold to wealthier neighborhoods as grass-fed or organic, or even advertised as antibiotic-free. The placement of several fast food chains within low-income communities of color ensures that the Black population is still given the "master's" scraps at higher rates than we are given the "master's" food.

What about "soul food," which is typically seen as the cultural cuisine of Black people in the U.S.? Although this is a cuisine that we find to be endearing and nostalgic, we need to recognize and unpack the fact that traditional soul food is an attachment to the industry of slavery. More than just recognize, we need to analyze these attachments within the context of the current health issues we face as a demographic, but also our understanding of food and culture. The soul food diet originates from the slave-master dynamic that prioritized the health, satisfaction, and dignity of white people, but also perpetuates the use of food access as a form of control. Soul food is the product of Black people transforming the scraps of society into meals for our families. Utilizing the "Black pollution" and "White purity" myth as a paradigm, we have historically been forced into accepting the leftover pieces of food; those pieces that the "master" deemed undesirable and unworthy of consumption by the white elite. Common dishes within the cuisine consist of pig intestine (chitterlings), pig feet, pig fat, and pig knuckle bone (ham hocks), clearly reflecting this process.

In contrast, decolonization refers to a process of unlearning the myths, stories, and history imposed upon us during colonization. Most importantly, it highlights the beauty of reconnecting to our culture and ourselves to our true history and roots before the white colonization of Black bodies, minds, and souls. The decolonize your diet movement is a call to action to reassess and reconnect with the diet inhabited by our ancestors, but most importantly, to disentangle the cultural narrative relating African American food and culture to unhealthy and gluttonous cuisine without acknowledging the impact of colonization on our customs. Specifically, scholars within this movement encourage the use of our ancestral Indigenous and African food and cuisine as medicine to prevent and alleviate the health disparities that result from the Standard U.S. American Diet, and ultimately, colonization. We aim to do so through a process of unlearning and relearning, and ultimately, a process of recreation and self-identification- of our cuisine and of our culture, but eventually, of our narrative.

Without the background analysis of the origins of soul food cuisine and the role colonization plays in our food, another cultural narrative persists that invalidates several social context issues related to food justice. This cultural narrative is the myth that Black people do not want to eat healthy, Black people are the origin and sustainer of our unhealthy cuisine, and we have a natural affinity to traditional soul food with no desire to change. With this narrative comes the familiar undertone that Black people are responsible for our own demise and have no real desire to change our habits. As people of color, especially vegans of color, we should think critically in order to read between those lines.

Failings of Healthful Foods Initiatives

A semi-experimental study on significant factors impeding upon food access and food sovereignty established a six-week program through the Alternative Food Network (AFN) that provided produce to low-income Black families through Hollygrove Market and Farm (HMF). An analysis of this semi-experimental study outlined a concept known as the *digital divide*. The concept refers to the use of web communication to spread the word about alternative food movements and reflects the general tendency of these locations to be white-dominated spaces. The study noted that while the first weeks of the program were successful, the declining rate of participants as the program continued was alarming. What the analysis brought to light was that while, initially, the market used physical flyers and announcements for its opening, most daily communication and operations tend to rely upon technology. With regards to food access, this digital divide is worth considering due to the decline in resident participation where 80% of study participants were ultimately uninformed about newer services such as Electronic Bank Transfer (EBT) acceptance, resident discounts and home delivery. Thus, having primarily used digital means of communication within communities that lag in consistent access to the web negatively impacted their ability to reap the benefits of this program.[10]

Furthermore, according to the study's analysis, mainstream AFNs tend to consider and study "food access as an outcome of individual choices rather than of structural impediments," which is dissimilar to food justice views and strategies. In actuality, the HMF study and analysis highlighted the importance of healthy neighborhood interventions to:

> 1. provide programming and marketing materials that are accessible to the specific community;
> 2. provide produce that is culturally relevant, such as collard greens, as opposed to bok choy; and
> 3. take time to consult the community to discover the factors preventing them from utilizing the resources;

Thus, it is inherently racist to impose blame upon the Black consumer for failing to consume healthier options without equitable education and awareness of one's transitioning food environment. Solutions to accessibility should include proactive discussions within this area of research to specifically address the multitude of reasons why Black people in low-income communities still *do* consume "junk food" at higher rates than healthier options. This analysis needs to be done at a social context level, rather than individual level, when we consider that individual consumer choices are not individual choices at all. Most importantly, food justice scholars must become well acquainted with the concept that our societal desire to blame the Black community for their lack of participation with a healthy corner store initiative program stems from inherently racist assumptions. In conclusion, one could say that the lack of participation on behalf of Black people actually says more about the lack of holistic and culturally aware food introductions and community engagement of healthy food initiatives. One example of the disconnect is the current pattern of introducing only expensive vegan snacks as an alternative to childhood favorites, such as a small bag of Hippeas for $1.95 compared to a large bag of Cheetos for $2.00. Adding to the lack of awareness, many healthy corner store initiatives require consumers to choose between a $10 salad and a $2 hot dog. Thus, most healthy options are introduced to low-income communities of color through nutritionally insufficient and otherwise unappealing, stereotypical healthy options, such as an apple and a salad. Ironically, they are then presented as the less convenient, less sustaining, yet more expensive option.

Healthful Foods: Representation & Impacts

Let's consider that wealthier, predominantly white neighborhoods have higher access the opportunity of exposure to a wider range of healthier, plant-based options, including vegan pizza, vegan burgers, or even, vegan wings, as well as cheese replacements and a wide variety of healthier plant milk while, as discussed, low-income Black communities receive less than appealing representations of alternatives to unhealthy foods. Within these contexts, the ability to veganize and create nutritious cuisines from white cultures (i.e. Italian, Greek, and French cuisines) is typically touted as a simple act, while purporting efforts of creating healthier alternatives of soul food as impossible. The reality is that healthy food initiatives must also take representation into account in order to make healthy food options appealing when introduced to specific communities, such as low-income Black communities and Latinx communities. Food is an important and often culturally identifying aspect across communities, and people of color should not be expected to admonish their history, traditional ingredients, and cultural cuisines for generic health salads or more prevalent white-based cuisines.

It is important for Black communities to know that healthy soul food is possible and already happening. The veganization of soul food is a way to reclaim and decolonize our bodies and customs, while re-empowering the meaning of African American culture. Based on this realization, Black vegans have begun to create and share veganized versions of soul food classics through restaurants and even in book form. An abundance of vegan soul food restaurants can be found in neighborhoods across the country, such as NuVegan Cafe and Evolve Vegan Restaurant, both located in Washington, DC; Souley Vegan in Oakland, CA; Soul Vegetarian South in Atlanta, GA; and Seasoned Vegan in Harlem, NY. Black vegan chefs have taken the initiative of creating cookbooks with the aim of introducing vegan soul food into family kitchens. Such works include that of Bryant Terry, author of the *Vegan Soul Kitchen: Fresh, Healthy, and Creative African-American Cuisine* and *Afro-Vegan: Farm-Fresh African, Caribbean, and Southern Flavors Remixed,* as well as the work of Atlanta-born Black chef Jenné Claiborne who authored the *Sweet Potato Soul* cookbook and Texas-born Black vegan chef Cametria Hill, which guides readers through the process of embracing plant-based diets, from shopping, tips, and accessible veganized Southern favorites, in her book, *A Southern Girl's Guide to Plant-Based Eating.*

Would the health status of Black people in the United States be any better if our access to grass-fed, organic and free-range animal products were to increase? Actually, the official position of the Academy of Nutrition and Dietetics expresses support for vegan diets as a nutritionally adequate intervention to the reduction of chronic disease.[11] Within the 2016 Journal of the Academy of Nutrition and Dietetics, plant-based diets were recognized as a healthful strategy in order to prevent, and even reverse, diet-related disease. As we know, the current health crisis of Black and Brown communities is largely due to diet-related diseases, but the abstract appropriately mentions that vegans are at a reduced risk of specific health conditions, such as type 2 diabetes, heart disease, hypertension and obesity. These are a few of the several health conditions that most significantly impact Black and Brown communities. According to this data, the health status of Black people in the United States would have the best opportunity to improve if access to veganism in our communities were to increase.

Therefore, higher access to grass-fed and/or farm-raised meat is *not* a part of the solution to food injustice.

To use animal foods as a solution to food injustice is an ironic method of addressing health disparities, which are rooted in environmental racism. Specifically, we only have to look at the irony in the introduction of grass-fed beef as a solution to health problems for Black people in the U.S. when we consider animal agriculture's impact on *water*. It takes 2,500 gallons of water to produce just 1 pound of U.S. beef and 1,000 gallons to produce 1 gallon of milk.[12] Yet, the people of Flint, a predominantly Black rural town in southern Michigan, have been without any clean water for over 1,300 days (longer by the time you read this). It is also important to mention that over 40 percent of Flint residents are experiencing poverty.[13] While we may feel hopeless in addressing the Flint Water Crisis, the truth is that someone who currently eats 1 pound of beef per day could save around 17,000 gallons of water by eliminating beef for just one week. In doing so, one could analyze policies that could speed up the process of reallocating the water supply in the United States for environmental equity. After all, 55 percent of all water consumed in the United States is used for animal agriculture.

When analyzing both of these social problems contextually, we can begin to adjust our lens to Black veganism as a form of protest and a food justice approach. In an attempt to be a holistic and thorough advocate for environmental justice, we have to evaluate the situation through an interdisciplinary lens.

Solutions That Work

Importantly, it is critical to note and to highlight that the integration of fresh produce and healthier options must be coupled with the exposure to nutrition education, produce knowledge, food justice discussion, and other forms of community-based engagement. Before imposing shame upon the consumer, one needs to truly analyze the difference between accessibility and affordability, but also, the several factors beyond individual preference that discourage Black consumer involvement with healthy corner store initiatives.

Social myths perpetuated through untold and/or misrepresented narratives from those looking from the outside-in must also be abolished. Fast food consumers are presumed to be careless, willfully ignorant, and beyond oncological repair. Those leading initiatives must be willing to unpack the problematic association of Black people with fast food consumption, and how this translates to gluttony and carelessness. By connoting fast food consumption with carelessness toward health and inability to suppress carnal desires, we create a myth of the fast food consumer as a poor Black person. This myth allows for Black food consumption to be controlled, regulated, and promulgated under the guise of individual choice.

Other solutions include the incorporation of workshops offering cooking classes, product awareness, resource guides, and nutrition education that are designed and executed by Black professionals that are aware of these hurdles and how-to prepare healthy plant-based alternatives based on culturally relevant dishes. It is important that we, as Black people, feel encouraged to adopt a vegan lifestyle even within harmful food environments. Black vegans with access to veganism have a responsibility to conduct research and facilitate discussions around the reason *why* healthy plant-based foods are inaccessible to most of the Black population in the United States. Black vegans could pioneer the effort to bring this same access, resources, and awareness to low-income Black communities through Black owned/operated businesses or organizations.

One example of an organization doing this is Fuel the People, a nonprofit organization with an initiative to serve, empower, and provide vegan awareness for the Black community in the Washington D.C. metropolitan area through free plant-based food distribution and food justice education programs. The main mission of the organization is to provide free vegan food distribution programs, conduct community garden projects, as well as raise awareness about Black veganism as a social justice movement and form of protest against our current food system. Fuel the People aims to offer education programs and seminars related to food justice, Black veganism, vegan activism, and food insecurity. Through food justice work, Fuel the People hopes to establish a high density of affordable and accessible plant-based food resources, restaurants, social groups, and educational opportunities that are for us, by us.

A Continuation of Colonialism?

People of color have been marginalized within the vegan movement to the point that the word itself is currently associated with whiteness. However, outside of the loudest majority, vegans of color exist, and Black vegans have taken the lead towards creating healthier, plant-based alternatives of traditional foods. As outlined in this essay, a vegan praxis *is* a practical solution. Yet some important questions remain that must be addressed in order to create a food justice plan that is aware and therefore, effective:

Why is the vegan lifestyle inaccessible to most Black people in the United States?

Why don't corner stores have vegan alternatives?

Why aren't food education classes available at Black and Brown community centers?

Why have we, as people of color, been placed on the margins of the vegan movement?

Why does the condition of poverty, coupled with a Black and/or Latinx identity, determine one's right to live healthfully?

In closing, we can reflect on the myths of the polluted and the pure to recognize the cyclic relationship between these myths and our food system. When we actively detangle Whiteness from a plant-based lifestyle and supreme health, we detangle Blackness from a fast food lifestyle and health-related conditions. Are veganism and plant-based diets a continuation of colonialism? No. If we look beyond an erroneously categorized, white-faced movement for a privileged majority, we see that the accessibility and implementation of Black veganism would mean alleviating communities of color from colonial-imposed health conditions and even issues like environmental racism. Through a Black vegan praxis, we can begin to relentlessly address race within the context of food justice.

Citations

1. Food Access Research Atlas: Documentation (2017). *United States Department of Agriculture Economic Research Service.*

2. Johns Hopkins Center for a Livable Future (2018). Healthy Food Priority Areas 2018.

3. The Grocery Gap Who Has Access to Healthy Food and Why It Matters (2015). 1st ed. [eBook].

4. United States Census Bureau (2016).

5. DC Hunger Solutions (2017). Closing the Grocery Gap in the Nation's Capital.

6. Centers for Disease Control and Prevention (2017). Health of Black or African American non-Hispanic Population. Retrieved February 13, 2018.

7. Centers for Disease Control and Prevention (2017). Health of Hispanic or Latino Population. Retrieved February 13, 2018.

8. Cooksey-Stowers, K.; Schwartz, M.B., and Brownell, K.D. (2017). Food Swamps Predict Obesity Rates Better Than Food Deserts in the United States. *International Journal of Environmental Research and Public Health*, 14, 1366.

9. Kwate, N. O. (2008). Fried chicken and fresh apples: Racial segregation as a fundamental cause of fast food density in black neighborhoods. Health & Place, 14(1), 32-44. doi:10.1016/j.healthplace.2007.04.001

10. Kato, Y. and McKinney, L. (2014). Bringing food desert residents to an alternative food market: a semi-experimental study of impediments to food access. Agriculture and Human Values, 32(2), 215-227. doi:10.1007/s10460-014-9541-3

11. Melina, V., Craig, W., and Levin, S. (2016). Position of the Academy of Nutrition and Dietetics: Vegetarian Diets. *Journal of the Academy of Nutrition and Dietetics, 116*(12), 1970-1980. doi:10.1016/j.jand.2016.09.025

12. Robbins, John. "2,500 gallons all wet?" Earth Save: Healthy People Healthy Planet.

13. Judge, M. (2017). #Flint: 1,299 Days of No Clean Water, but State Advisory Committee Says, "Nothing to Discuss." Accessed February 13, 2018.

CHAPTER SEVEN

Veganic Farming

By Helen Atthowe

One of the best ways to bring justice into the world starts with what we put on our plates every day. The way we grow our food and the farming practices we support when we purchase food make a huge difference to the lives of animals and other organisms with whom we share this planet. An important part of being kind to animals and respectful of our environment is educating ourselves about how different farming practices treat other humans, animals and the land. When we choose to practice and/or support veganic farming, we expand the concept of "social justice" to include more and more living creatures. The umbrella under which we place what we care about spreads even larger and fills with even more life. Feeding ourselves becomes an act of connecting with the world around us, as well as developing compassionate awareness that, over time, makes us better and happier humans.

Veganic farming is a way of sustaining ourselves without contributing to the death of other living beings. It is about nonviolence to the earth, animals, birds, insects, amphibians, and to ourselves. This type of farming is a willingness to balance our existence with the natural world. This balancing includes an awareness of the soil microorganisms we try not to disturb with excessive tillage; the birds, butterflies, and insects we do not poison with insecticides; the weeds that are not killed with herbicides; and the animals who are not killed for food or fertilizer. Simply stated, veganic farming works with nature, rather than against it, and empowers humans to be a part of that whole.

Veganic farming uses no synthetic pesticides, no artificial fertilizers, and no Genetically Modified Organisms. In addition, unlike organic farming, veganic farming *does not* use animal manure, animal bodies, or animal parts (such as fertilizers made from bone meal, blood meal, feather meal or liquefied fish bodies). Instead, veganic farms are designed as complex systems, where natural ecosystem functions are encouraged, and native animals, birds, and insects are welcome. Biological control of insect and disease pests occurs naturally by creating or maintaining habitat for pest-eating birds, bats, insects, fungi, bacteria, and soil microorganisms.

Veganic farming mimics natural plant ecosystems with three main foci:

Reduced tillage. Veganic farms try to keep the soil covered with plants throughout the growing season and over the winter. Most other farms till the soil regularly each growing season to incorporate fertilizers and to control weeds.

Increased plant diversity. Practicing diversity means growing many kinds of crops in the same field, growing non-crop living mulches (such as clover) with crops, and allowing certain weeds to remain in fields.

Regular addition of plant residues. Plant residues are used as fertilizers and are added to the soil in two ways: to the soil surface and/or incorporated into the soil. Plant residue fertilizers include: chipped branch wood mulches, mowed clover and grass living mulches, and alfalfa meal (see list of veganic fertilizers below).

Plant-Based Soil Management

Something notable of veganic farming is its implementation of plant-based soil management. Many farmers believe that animals and their manure are essential for healthy soils and crop production, but that is not necessarily true. Every time I walk through the woods, I marvel at how native forests keep growing and producing all of that biomass without anyone adding fertilizer to "boost production." Forests are sustainably fertile, yet the average density of wild animals per acre within forest ecosystems is much lower than that of most animal-based farms. Forest nutrient cycling and soil fertility is based mainly on plants: their complex interactions with soil microbes, their death, decay, and recycling of nutrients back to the soil. This kind of plant-based, high-carbon soil fertility system is the foundation upon which veganic soil management is built.

The reason that most organic farmers use manure is

because it is a relatively rapid plant-available source of the nutrients crop plants need most. Manure supplies large quantities of nitrogen, phosphorus, and potassium. However, while the plant nutrients in manure become available to crops quickly, they can also quickly be lost to leaching during rainy weather and when farms irrigate heavily.

However, there are several environmental and human health problems with manure:

- It produces greenhouse gas (such as methane and nitrous oxide).
- Rapid nitrogen and phosphorus release can result in surface and ground water nitrate and phosphate pollution problems, such as *eutrophication* of surface water (explosive algal growth due to excessive nutrients, which depletes the water of oxygen when the algae die). Excessive levels of nitrate in groundwater are suspected in instances of blood poisoning in infants and stomach cancer in older persons.
- Manures from non-organic farm animals may contain antibiotics and pesticides. There are human health risks associated with consumption of fresh vegetables grown in soil amended with antibiotic-laden manures.[1]
- Manures may contain human pathogens, such as *Salmonella* and *Escherichia coli.* Cattle were found to be the primary pool of *E. coli* in the environment[2, 3] and this pathogen was found in vegetables grown in manure-fertilized soils.[4]

Veganic fertilizers are plant- or mineral-based and contain slower-to-release plant-available nutrients. *Nitrogen-fixing legumes* are one of the main tools in the veganic soil management toolbox. They are used as "green manures," cover crops, and living mulches. Green manures and cover crops are normally incorporated into the soil with tillage in the spring, before crops are planted. Living mulches are not tilled, but grow in between crops and are periodically mowed to add plant residues back to the soil. Legumes can provide as much nitrogen (N), phosphorous (P), and potassium (K) as animal products and manures, usually without such a rapid release that nitrogen or phosphorus pollution occur. Good examples are clovers, alfalfa, medics, beans and Austrian field peas.

Depending on soil type and health, when temperatures are warm (greater than 50°F) and soil moisture is adequate, legume green manures and cover crops can provide nutrients for crops approximately 2-3 weeks after being tilled into the soil, as well as throughout the growing season. A healthy soil is one that has a good balance of plant nutrients (especially N, P, and K), at least 3% organic matter, and a diverse community of soil microorganisms that help to keep soils fertile.

Here are some examples of veganic fertilizers and the nutrients they provide:

- Soybean/cottonseed/alfalfa meal – mostly for N, also P and K
- Seaweed – K, minerals, micronutrients
- Wood ash – K
- Lime – Calcium (Ca)
- Epsom salts - Magnesium
- Basalt rock/rock powders – P
- Gypsum – Sulfur and Ca
- Chipped branch wood (made from deciduous tree

branches that are under 2 ½ inches in diameter) – Adds carbon to increase soil's organic matter and feed soil microorganisms.
- Local carbon sources, such as yard waste compost, spent hops from breweries, and leaves that can be composted or used as mulch.

Farming and gardening using veganic techniques requires attention to biological details, and depends on several factors you can't change much and need to work with:

- Climate, which includes precipitation, humidity, and sun exposure (full sun/shade and south or north-facing slopes).
- Soil type (*sand, clay, loam*). Loamy soils are best for gardening. Sandy soils have poor nutrient and water holding potential. Heavy clay soils hold too much water and don't allow enough oxygen for plant roots.
- Seasonal temperatures (high, low, and average temperatures).
- Climate types (dry/hot summers or summers with hot days and cold nights, rainy/wet winters or cold/freezing winters).

Undertaking Veganic Farming

Veganic farming has been successfully applied to both small and large-scale growing operations. Farms such as phillyGrown.farm in Philadelphia, Pennsylvania; Woodleaf Farm in Richland, Oregon; and Awali Veganic Homestead Education Center in Stone Mountain, Georgia use veganic farming to grow crops such as mushrooms, hazelnuts, peaches, and a wide variety of other fruits, vegetables, and nuts. In the U.S. at least, veganic farms vary in size from small, family-run operations to medium-sized, educational-use plots to large-scale commercial operations.[5] This type of farming can also be found in a myriad of other countries worldwide, including Belize, Canada, India, Ireland, Switzerland, and the U.K.[6]

There are many ways in which veganic farming can also be applied within a wide range of individual spaces, from balcony gardens to smaller plots. The most important aspect of implementing this type of system is knowing where to start and understanding the local climate and soil types available to work with. There are many basic gardening and soil management articles online and in books that provide a more in-depth understanding of which crops are best to grow in particular soil types and climates, and how to ameliorate climate and soil challenges (for example, shading in a hot climate to cool crops like Brussels sprouts that like cool nights, or floating row covers in a cold climate for tomatoes that need protection from frost). GoVeganic.Net is one such valuable resource to use as a starting point for anyone who wants to attempt veganic farming. The site features handy tips and lists, as well as articles describing different methods of at-home veganic farming and applications, including advice on plants to start with depending on the region.

In getting started, you will need to spend some time planning your garden to fit it into your climate and soil type. An easy, do-it-yourself test to find your soil type is available from Michigan-Garden.Com. Upon knowing what kind of soil you have to work with in order to make it as suitable as needed, something to note is that soil fertility is a biological detail that can be easily influenced.

Aspects of soil fertility that are moldable are:

- Level of "soil organic matter." This is the framework and "biological skeleton" of soil; it is the home and food source for all the soil microorganisms that comprise the soil foodweb.
- Soil pH, which affects the soil's ability to provide nutrients and feed your plants.
- Levels and balance of N, P, K, Calcium, and micronutrients such as sulfur, zinc, and manganese that plants need to grow and stay healthy.

Mulch, vegetable compost, green manure, chipped branch wood, and other plant-based fertility techniques are all ways to replace animal derived ones.[7]

Beyond substrate, some other basic factors to keep in mind when starting to implement veganic methods are the size of the available growing space and light availability. Learning about the different types of systems that can be implemented within your specific bioregion and parameters is also a good place to start. For example, container gardening allows people to grow in small, indoor spaces such as apartments, as well as in places where soil is contaminated.[8] This is probably somewhat familiar to you already, as the "method" really just means "to grow plants in containers rather than in the ground." Still, it is worth looking into the types of containers you can get, the types of soil that you can use, and so forth (You may even want to experiment with creating your own containers!). Another system known as the Ruth Stout method is a technique in which soil is never tilled; instead, soil quality is entirely dependent on *mulching*. The method consists of keeping a thick layer of hay mulch permanently on the soil. This can be summed up as the "law of least effort." Nature does most of the work.[9] While Ruth Stout did not invent this method, as it has been happening organically around the world since time immemorial, she was the first to write extensively about the topic, and her work influenced many ecological gardeners.

An alternative technique that is similarly hands-off is the cultivation of self-fertilizing gardens— ones that use the "synergistic gardening" approach, developed by Emilia Hazelip. After establishing the garden, there is no further tilling, and no use of external inputs such as fertilizers and pesticides. Instead, soil health is maintained by the selection of plants, mulching (like the Ruth Stout method, by which Emilia Hazelip was influenced), and recycling of plant residues.[10, 11] There are several more techniques that are worth looking into in an effort to work with what you have available.

Whichever way you decide to start your journey into veganic farming, you will be joining other individuals taking a step towards a revolutionary way of gardening and farming that is a versatile and customizable way of growing food. On a larger-scale, we can approach and work with local community leaders in an effort to raise awareness of systems like this, which take care to work with local biotic and abiotic factors, to implementing changes to the way food is grown. Collectively, we can attempt to implement this novel concept of community nourishment in a way that respects and works with the environment to minimize harm for all.

Citations

1. K. Kumar, S. C. Gupta, S. K. Baidoo, V. Chandera and C. J. Rosena. 2005. "Antibiotic uptake by plants from soil fertilized with animal manure." *Journal of Environmental Quality*, 34:2082-2085 DOI: 10.2134/jeq2005.0026

2. Cobbold, R. and Desmarchelier, P. 2000. "A longitudinal study of Shiga-toxigenic Escherichia coli (STEC) prevalence in three Australian dairy herds." *Veterinary Microbiology,* 71, 125–137

3. Ogden, I.D., MacRae, M. and Strachan, N.J.C. 2004. "Is the prevalence and shedding concentrations of E. coli O157 in beef cattle in Scotland seasonal?" *FEMS Microbiology Letters* 233, 297–300.

4. Ingham, S.C., J.A. Losinski, M.P. Andrews, J.E. Breuer, J.R. Breuer, T.M. Wood, and T.H. Wright. 2004. "*Escherichia coli* contamination of vegetables grown in soils fertilized with noncomposted bovine manure: garden-scale studies." *Applied Environmental Microbiology*, 70:6420-6427.

5. "Mapping Veganic Farms in the United States." *Veganic World.* Accessed May 3, 2018.

6. "Find a Farm." *Veganic World.* Accessed May 3, 2018.

7. "Introduction to Veganics." *Go Veganic.* Accessed May 8, 2018.

8. "Approaches to Veganic." *Go Veganic.* Accessed May 5, 2018.

9. "The Ruth Stout System of Permanent Hay Mulching." *Go Veganic.* Accessed May 5, 2018.

10. Ibid.

11. "Synergistic gardening." Wikipedia entry. Accessed May 5, 2018.

CHAPTER EIGHT

Teachable Moments

By Saryta Rodriguez, Starr Carrington, and Michelle Carrera

With respect to any social justice movement, there are (at least) two primary forms of knowledge one can attain and utilize in order to strengthen one's work: theoretical knowledge, based on history and social science; and practical knowledge, based on actually doing the work. While some of the previous chapters, such as "Case Study and Interview: Occupy the Farm," speak to the latter, I thought it would be helpful to include a chapter that focused specifically on Teachable Moments: moments from the careers of people who have worked in food justice in one way or another that taught them valuable lessons about what the movement needs in order to be successful. Below, you will find four such experiences: two of my own; one by Starr Carrington, founder of Fuel the People, a nonprofit organization devoted to solving the hunger crisis in Washington D.C. while promoting veganism; and one by Michelle Carrera, founder of Chilis on Wheels, a nonprofit organization that serves vegan food to those in need in Puerto Rico, New York City and other cities across the U.S.

Teachable Moment #1

It Takes a Village
By Saryta Rodríguez

As the fall semester of my senior year at Columbia University rolled around, I, like many of my peers, found myself struggling with What Comes Next. I did not, as many of my peers did, have an internship during college, as I was a Work Study student. Rather than spending my summers being trained in a practical skill set by a company that would undoubtedly hire me upon graduation, provided I didn't fuck up in spectacular fashion, I spent them alternating between visiting my family on Long Island and working on campus, saving my money for books, Metrocards, and, yes, the cigarettes and booze of which New York college students are so regrettably fond of. Having majored in Sociology and Philosophy (or "concentrated," as I believe Columbia calls it), I did not have a straightforward career path to follow. The world was my ashtray, and it was at once liberating and terrifying.

One of the first opportunities I considered at the time was joining Teach for America, a nonprofit organization dedicated to placing new, highly qualified teachers in low-income school districts in an effort to close the education gap that has plagued the U.S. for far too long. I applied, made it through Rounds 1 and 2, and was invited to Round 3: a final, group interview at which I was expected to listen, discuss, and finally, present a five-minute teaching lesson on the subject, and for the academic grade of my choice. This last part of the application made me the most anxious, but, in the end, it needn't have; I ultimately decided before even giving my presentation that I would not pursue a position with this organization.

Before I get into the Why, I'd like to clarify that what follows is by no means a condemnation of Teach for America. Although this was a real experience that happened to me, the experience may have been tainted by any of a number of factors. I cannot say with certainty that what I was told by this one facilitator, at this one interview round, in this one city, in this one state, and, now, nearly a decade ago, was even standard practice for the organization as a whole *at that time*, much less today.

I certainly hope not.

A group of roughly twenty to twenty-five bright-eyed, bushy-tailed, do-gooder college seniors such as myself piled into a conference room somewhere in lower Manhattan. We started off as the audience of a lecture; our facilitator introduced herself and proceeded to lay out some Dos and Don'ts of teaching in low-income school districts, alongside other introductory information. I remember her saying something about how, even though many of the children we would be serving suffered from food insecurity, it was not our job to feed these children, but only to teach them. She waxed poetic about the various methods and strategies for effective teaching that can be employed for any student, regardless of race, socioeconomics, or any other factors. If memory serves, she may have even handed out one of those fact sheets that lists all the different types of learners there are: verbal or "reading/writing" learners, such as myself; auditory learners, kinetic (tactile/requiring physical manipulation of objects) learners, and so forth.

My gut lurched in my belly at this. I felt instinctively that it was wrong.

My mother has been a teacher in low-income schools on Long Island since I was maybe ten or eleven years old. I'd listened to the many stories she told about her students' suffering and how she strove to alleviate it— not by pretending that hunger wasn't there, but by offering snacks in her classroom (many, if not all, of which she paid for out-of-pocket) and speaking about hunger and other social issues with fellow teachers and school administrators. Later, when I joined City Year New York, I would find myself and the team I led at P.S. 57 engaging in similar behavior in order to meet the needs of the children we served so that they would be receptive to what we taught them, and neither distracted nor demoralized by hunger.

Aside from this vicarious experience I had with the issue, on a more common-sense level, I just thought it truly impossible to expect a starving person to learn anything. Even as a reasonably privileged, well-fed child, I myself found that I sometimes had trouble concentrating in whatever class I had just before lunchtime, as I grew hungrier from years of having adapted to eating something every weekday at noon or one p.m. as a public school elementary student. That was just a result of being *slightly hungry*— not starving. How can a truly starving child be expected to concentrate on anything other than their own desire for food?

I kept my mouth shut. I still wanted the job, and I figured these were guidelines, not rules. I doubted anyone would fire me for attempting to address hunger issues among my future students, and I still doubt that.

Soon thereafter, it was time for us to break into groups.

Each group was given a sheet with hypothetical situations (or maybe just one at a time; I don't recall, and you'll see why momentarily) and asked to discuss how to address them. Coincidentally, the either sole or first situation with which my working group was presented had to do with hunger. I used this opportunity to address my concerns about what we'd been told with the group, assuming naively that at least one person would take my point. If they did, they didn't speak up about it. Instead, two group members took turns parroting what our facilitator had said. As the facilitator passed by our group on her eavesdropping expedition about the room, she gave one of them an approving look.

So, I left.

I was crestfallen. To see so many well-intentioned and capable young people in that room, on the brink of charging forth into communities that did not at all resemble their own, doomed to failure because they simply could not appreciate the scope of the issues their students would face on a daily basis— and were not being encouraged to do so by the sole organization representative in the room— was disheartening. It really drove home this idea to me that there is no shortage of good people in this country; people *want* to be good. People *want* to do the right thing. But when you come from a place of privilege— a home in which the question was always, "What's for dinner?" and never "Is there dinner?"; in which you went home from school every day knowing that your father would not be beating your mother and that no one would beat you; in which your parents were never afraid to pick up the phone or answer the doorbell and risk being deported— and you endeavor to place yourself in a disadvantaged, oppressed, struggling place and make it better, you have to understand *why it is struggling in the first place.*

It's not because all of their teachers are terrible. It's not because their parents don't love them. It's because aspects of our society, such as systemic racism, systemic sexism, and income inequality— all of which are inextricably linked— have left these communities, and many of the households therein, broken and in desperate need of both short-term, hands-on assistance and long-term socioeconomic empowerment.

The primary concern of an educator is to educate, just as the primary concern of a chef is to cook, and the primary concern of a doctor is to provide medical care. That said, a good chef knows about things like allergies, veganism, seasonality, and gluten intolerance— not just how to prepare food five different ways. Similarly, a good educator must know the basic conditions in which their students live and in which they arrive to the classroom— not just how to teach five different ways.

It truly does take a village to raise a happy, healthy and educated child. The most intelligent, motivated and kindhearted teacher cannot hope to make a profound impact on their students if those students are starving and no one cares because "It's not a school's job to feed kids, but only to teach them." Compartmentalizing hunger and expecting it to be resolved is like trying to compartmentalize systemic racism, saying "Only racial justice advocates should care; the rest of us can just ignore it." Hunger, like systemic racism, permeates every aspect of the hungry person's life— including academic performance. In order to achieve food justice on a national level, let alone on an international level, we must *all* embrace this as our calling. It is *all* of our jobs to feed our children.

Teachable Moment #2

Teach by Living It
By Starr Carrington

Since I was a little girl, my favorite food has always been mac and cheese. My grandma's classic recipe stole my heart from an early age, and I will never forget the moment when she passed that recipe onto me. As a vegetarian, I was able to continue enjoying that classic recipe during holidays and, in fact, I found solace in that for a long time. Because while I may have missed out on the ham, the turkey and the ribs- I would always have my mac and cheese.

Before going vegan, I believed that I could just never give it up - especially not my grandmother's recipe. What I know now is that there is a vegan substitute for every single ingredient in that classic recipe I've always adored. After becoming acquainted with vegan YouTubers, I learned that condensed milk can be swapped for condensed almond milk, and that there is a plethora cheddar, American, and mozzarella cheeses at my fingertips that melt just as beautifully. This past holiday season, I created a veganized, baked mac and cheese of my grandma's classic recipe and the whole family was surprised at the recreation of flavor, and of culture.

A salient turning point for me was my first visit to NuVegan Cafe. I ordered the fried chik'n wings, mac & cheese and collard greens. I distinctly remember thinking; if this is what vegan food tastes like, I could do this. I often wonder how different my journey would be without this experience, because it was the first time that I saw veganism represented within my culture. Had I never known about this integration of veganism and soul food, I probably would not have opened up my mind to learning more about transitioning.

As a Black vegan, this is why I take the initiative to share even the smallest part of my journey that I think could serve as a turning point in one's understanding of veganism. For example, as a person who has access to veganism, the only thing holding me back from opening my mind to transitioning was the classic mac and cheese. For someone else, this may be fried chik'n- which is offered at vegan soul food restaurants throughout the country and can be recreated at home.

I've learned to view everything that I do, as a Black feminist vegan, as a teachable moment. Throughout my journey, my friends and family have always asked questions regarding veganism or food justice work to which I felt unequipped to respond. I was under the impression that I needed statistics, evidence and documentaries on my side in order to introduce veganism to my immediate community. Shortly after making a full transition to veganism, I decided to make informative YouTube videos about the role of veganism as a way to address the social issues that Black and Latinx communities endure. While the original intention was to provide uncomfortable truths that would guilt my community into further considering veganism, I ended up posting more recipe videos than anything else. After posting several photos and recipe videos of vegan comfort foods, I finally began to connect with a non-vegan audience, and I realized what had been missing from my advocacy before: education.

By posting vegan fried chik'n, macaroni and cheeze, greens, jerk eggplant and beefless Jamaican patties, among other things, I was able to acquire and maintain a large non-vegan following that consists of people of color. It was then that I realized that, as a vegan of color, every moment we live in a non-vegan world is an experience from which non-vegans can learn. They want to know how you navigate family gatherings, social outings and late-night cravings while maintaining and encouraging a vegan lifestyle. Just by making a bowl of cereal with almond milk and corn pops, I've heard feedback from friends and supporters about how they have felt inspired to transition from cow's milk to a plant-based milk alternative. I also learned Black people with access to veganism are discouraged from adopting this lifestyle by different factors, such as negative social impacts, cultural sacrifice, and general lack of knowledge.

What changed was the primary audience of my activism: people of color with access to veganism. I wanted to encourage them not only to begin their vegan journey, but also to question, analyze and, eventually, confront and restructure the current food system that is in place. My platform now serves as a resource to people of color, vegan and non-vegan alike, who want to learn more about vegan activism, expand the body of vegan resources for people of color and become involved in food justice solutions. I learned that Black people don't just want to hear about veganism or food justice. My community is attached to foods that we have been conditioned to love and believe that veganism is a threat to the fulfillment that comes from the social and cultural elements of soul food. We want to know not only *why* we should live a vegan lifestyle on a daily basis but also *how* to do so at each point in the decision-making process. Generally, we are willing to learn how veganism could make a significant impact on communities of color, but we also want to know why we should give up cultural staples in order to effectively do so. Once others understand how you, as an example, live and operate within social and cultural situations on a daily basis, they will be encouraged to adopt some of your tips, tricks, recipes and practices.

To address the concern of how the focus on vegan recipes could minimize the importance of the nonhuman perspective, it is important to recognize recipes as an introduction. As a multidimensional resource, I've found a way to connect with people at each point of their transition, and I've noticed that the guilt I once sought to instill within people was not conducive to a conscious and encouraged transition. Sharing how one would go about living vegan on a daily basis serves as a tool to answer the initial question of: "What do I do next?"

While I post material on daily food and products, I also recently facilitated a breakout session on Environmental Racism at the 2018 RO(U)TES Social Justice Conference. The conference consisted of undergraduate- and graduate-level students who are oriented toward social justice scholarship and/or student activism. In the session, I asked the audience what it thought about vegan activism, and specifically encouraged *honesty*. Several students expressed, or agreed with, the sentiment that white vegans care more about nonhuman animal lives than human lives. This allowed me to realize how the overwhelmingly hypocritical narratives that stem from white veganism actually create a distance between the nonhuman perspective and people of color. This distance often prevents us from truly understanding the importance of the nonhuman perspective in one's vegan journey— which reinforces the significance of representation in the vegan movement.

While the session expounded upon the concretization of institutional racism within our food systems, we also discussed the perspective of nonhuman animals as it relates to the history of enslaved Black people. We also mentioned the association of veganism with expensive foods, and how that affects the reception of veganism within communities of color. I noticed that it is extremely helpful to debunk the myth that a cheap vegan lifestyle must mean rice and beans through this revitalization and reclaiming of soul food and other cultural cuisines. By acknowledging the substitutes that exist for animal products, especially those that seem essential to our culture, we can help diffuse this association of veganism with expensive food.

As I continue my journey, I have found it effective to strike a balance of relaying the nonhuman perspective that recognizes the historical and present struggle of Black people in the United States. However, as I serve to be an educational resource to people of color, I also hope to provide guidance and assistance that recognizes the daily steps of one's transition. At the beginning of my journey, I constantly looked to recipe videos that specifically represented my cultural cuisine in order to boost my confidence in the ethical decision I made. It is essential to provide the advice and tools that I've gained from my experience that allow me to sustain myself with a vegan lifestyle *as well as* the information and education that taught me the ethical significance of veganism.

I've found that vegan activism can be as complex as an

infographic analysis of the U.S. American state policies on Black health, or as simple as sharing a bowl of cereal. Use your platform to share the way you live your truth and your activism day by day. Share any and everything about your lifestyle; especially the parts that have become so mundane that you hardly recognize them, like that bowl of cereal. That is what we need the most.

Teachable Moment #3

Hold the Line
By Michelle Carrera

I was born, raised, and educated in Puerto Rico. Sixteen years ago, I looked at our pet rooster and couldn't fathom eating another animal or animal secretion. In the last fourteen years that I have been living in the United States, I was able to start Chilis on Wheels, which provides vegan food to people in need of a warm meal. We are essentially a vegan soup kitchen, and we have grown to include chapters in a couple of different cities throughout the country. We have expanded our services to include a Free Store, hold clothing drives, serve dog food for those who cannot provide for their animal companions, provide vegan education through talks and demos, and engage children to participate in their communities compassionately and in solidarity with their neighbors. Everything about starting Chilis on Wheels happened organically.

On Thanksgiving of 2014, I wanted my then 4-year-old son to volunteer in helping his community. Unfortunately, upon a Google search, we found out there were no vegan soup kitchens in the city. So, we did it ourselves. We made 15 meals in my little pots and walked the streets and gave out the food. Something about seeing people eat so fast, because they were truly hungry, made me think, "well, what about the other 364 days of the year?" I vowed to do more and increased that amount to once a month, but again it didn't feel significant. Once more, I then increased it again to once a week. Once we were at once a week, I could no longer afford to do it myself, so I turned to supermarkets to help me with donations. However, they all said that I had to be a registered tax-exempt nonprofit to be able to donate to me. So, I went ahead and did that. I downloaded the forms from the internet and did it on my own following all the steps required. And each step of the way has been the same; I am presented with a challenge, and I face it head on, wherever it may take us.

In the aftermath of Hurricane Maria in Puerto Rico, Chilis on Wheels was able to provide vegan food relief. In one month, we served 10,000 vegan meals and supplied people with 500 bags of groceries, water filters, solar lanterns, insect repellent, and other personal care items—while advocating for veganism at the same time.

I came to Puerto Rico because I could not stop the call of the heart. I listened through the storm's passing on the only radio station operating online. Hour after hour after hour, as devastation after devastation was reported. I could not stop sobbing and pacing. This was the land that gave me life, that sustained me; the land where I was shaped as an adult. This wasn't some distant, exotic, palm-tree-margarita-beach town. This had been home. The only real home I had ever known.

Whenever I find heartbreak in my life, I try to find a solution. I'm a doer. When something is broken, you fix it. Or you realize that you'll never be able to fix it, but someone someday might; so, you just hold the line until someone comes along who'll be able to redeem all the work you've put into it.

I saw a lot of this in Puerto Rico in the few days after the storm, metaphorically as well as literally. People holding up fallen trees from on top of roofs and cars, until someone with a machete would come by and chop it to pieces. The work that we do in any justice movement is push until it can't be pushed any more, and then wait. You wait for the next generation, but you can't let up or you'll lose the legacy of all those who came before us.

There's a great deal of faith in that wait. You have to trust that you will be provided for, that the right opportunities will come along, that the people in different communities will accept you, that the people will step up to join you and help too, that the right person will show up, that "the great arch of the moral universe will bend towards justice." You have to trust in the direction your heart takes you. You have to believe that even if you aren't successful, your impact will be significant.

A few weeks after the storm, when it was already out of the media cycle, some agencies began pulling out, a new normal arose: life without power, with limited internet, with fewer businesses open, with 250,000 less Puerto Ricans on the island after the massive emigration. It became apparent that relief work is temporary, but rebuilding required replanting— really working at the roots. After a category 5 storm, it wasn't enough to give out 10,000 or 15,000 meals and leave. For change to be meaningful, it has to be transformative.

This is how the next chapter of my activism came to be. The idea for the Vegan Community Center came, and I decided that I needed to move to Puerto Rico permanently, return to my homeland, and establish ourselves there. We collaborate with local vegan businesses and bloggers, with the orphanages, nursing homes, and communities that we served food to in the aftermath of the hurricane. We rented a house to serve as our collective space, and we organize events and workshops, reaching out to some folks I have known all my life, and cold call those I don't know. We went ahead with the plan without knowing if it would work out. We follow our heart regardless of the outcome. Gratefully, it was meant to be, and within a month or two of being on the island we received an Impact Grant from The Pollination Project, and a programmatic grant from Unidos por Puerto Rico, which helps us with the costs of the meals we share a few times a week, and the workshops we hold in the space. The idea is to serve as a meeting point for diverse communities in its purpose of building and serving the community, while advocating for veganism, with sustainability as a guiding point in our new reality of climate change. We continue serving vegan food to vulnerable communities, we hold movie nights (documentaries), vegan cooking classes for adults and children, workshops on growing our own food, collecting rain water, building and repairing DIY solar panels, and even purifying our own water. All through a lens of veganism, of justice for ourselves, justice for the animals, and building the interpersonal relationships necessary to carry us through the bigger and worst storms that will come as this planet reaches its demise.

It is transformative change because when we are placed with the task of helping others, when we are suddenly an integral part of a community, our lives change in that moment and we become instruments of change ourselves.

We are significant. The future is bleak, but the quality of our communities, of our people, isn't.

Teachable Moment #4

Solidarity or Bust
By Saryta Rodríguez

John Sanbonmatsu's *The Postmodern Prince: Critical Theory, Left Strategy, and the Making of a New Political Subject*, outlines precisely why it is that the Left cannot survive in its current form— scattered single-issue movements competing for resources and attention— but instead must unite under a common umbrella of Justice if it is to succeed as a movement.[1] This idea is often described within the context of *intersectionality*, an approach to social issues which examines the intersections of personal identity and how various factors of one's identity yield specific types of oppression under the prevailing socioeconomic system of the United States. While many think of intersectionality as a new "buzzword" or fad, Kimberlé Crenshaw coined the term in 1989,[2] when examining the intersection of race and gender to determine that, contrary to the popular statement that "women make 79 cents for every dollar men make" in the U.S., only *white* women make this much;[3] for every white-man dollar, Black women make 63 cents,[4] Hispanic women make 54 cents,[5] Native women make 57 cents,[6] and so on.

Unfortunately, all too often I have witnessed the term *intersectionality* being used as a synonym for *diversity*. In my essay, "Intersectionality vs. Diversity: A Note to Vegan Organizations," which is included in the Introduction to *Veganism in an Oppressive World,*[7] I highlight the fact that a group can be *diverse* in terms of having a variety of people in it, but that same group of people may:

A) Be diverse in some ways, but not in others (i.e. racially diverse, but not gender-diverse), and/or
B) Fail to adopt an intersectional approach to societal problem solving, *independent of any apparent diversity amongst its members.*

I was once told by a leader of an activist group of which I was a part of that ours was *not* an intersectional organization. I had informed him that countless others were accusing our organization of claiming to be intersectional without actually being so; concerns had been raised, for instance, about the imagery we employed to promote our cause and the way some of our members had spoken to vegans of color. I was supremely disappointed to hear not only that he did not take this complaint seriously, dismissing my real-time account of what was going on by citing data gleaned from an iPad, but also that, rather than arguing that these complaints were false or unfounded, this person instead effectively told me that intersectionality was not important to the organization. He conveyed to me that its focus was squarely on the rights and liberties of *nonhuman* animals.

"I don't think we are really an intersectional organization, and I don't think anyone really thinks we promote ourselves as such," he told me, basing this analysis on the number of times the word "intersectionality" had appeared on our blog in the past few months.

Imagine my surprise when, some weeks later, a conference is held at which this same leader, addressing a room of anywhere from seventy-five to one hundred people, led the room in a round of applause for how intersectional it was!

Leaving aside for the moment that, in the literal sense, a room full of people cannot be intersectional— because intersectionality denotes a *process or strategy*, rather than a *quality or trait*— I found this statement highly problematic. Not only did it directly contradict what I had been told just weeks earlier (which meant that either I had been lied to then or that roughly a hundred people were being lied to presently), but it also had been prompted by simply looking around the room and seeing "diversity."

In that same room myself, while I did see and was grateful to be in the company of some folks from other countries, I also observed that the crowd was still majority white, majority cis (identifying with the gender one was assigned at birth), majority straight and majority "young-ish" (folks in their 20s and early 30s). That's not to say that this group of people wasn't capable of doing an abundance of good for the world. That's simply to say that even on the diversity level, I didn't see what others claimed to see— both the speaker and the 99.9% of the room that participated in this self-congratulatory applause.

Let's be extra generous now and suppose I *had* seen an abundance of diversity. This still wouldn't imply that, when marginalized persons have an idea or feedback for the group, leadership listens and makes adjustments based on what it hears. Similarly, even a group that grants this courtesy to its own members may fail to take into account sincere feedback from the public (and by sincere, I mean offered in a constructive spirit; a nonvegan telling vegans to "Shut up and go eat some carrots" is not sincere feedback).

Sitting quietly and taking notes is easy enough; actively changing course based on what others have said is more challenging— and far more important.

Unfortunately, the scattered movements of the Left have made minimal progress in recent years in adopting true intersectionality and still, much like the modern U.S. American workplace, prioritize acquiring a *diversity* of members over adopting *intersectionality* in their operational approaches. For example:

a) In October 2016, in the wake of the release of Donald Trump's recorded conversation with Billy Bush before an airing of *Access Hollywood* in 2005, in which he brags of committing various acts of sexual assault with impunity, PETA spread a meme with a photo of a kitten that read "Grab a Pussy!" in order to promote an adoption event.[8] This conveyed to me a chilling disregard by PETA for the tremendous trauma experienced by women who have been sexually assaulted by the United State's current president, as well as women everywhere who were reminded of their own experiences with sexual assault as a result of the Access Hollywood tape. This is but one of many ways in which PETA has historically promoted sexism (including encouraging women— and some men, but mostly women— to strip naked "for the animals"[9]); but it is the first instance I personally recall of the organization actively promoting *rape culture*, sexism's more sinister offspring.

b) In August 2015, Direct Action Everywhere (DxE) put out a siren call for activists to move to Berkeley and other areas that are already vegan-friendly in order to create "activist hubs," starting with an article by founder and Bay Area organizer Wayne Hsiung, which originally ended with an unequivocal demand: "Move to Berkeley."[10] (Some posts are edited multiple times after publication, so this particular ending may no longer appear on DxE's website.) As I explain in my essay, "'Move to Berkeley!' and Other Follies" (found in *Veganism in an Oppressive World)*, such a call is extremely uninviting to activists who cannot afford to pay the sky-high rents of Berkeley, as well as those who cannot move for other reasons, such as taking care of a sick and/or elderly relative. Statistically, persons of color are at once more likely to be of low income in the U.S. *and* more likely to be responsible for sick and/or elderly relatives than white people, rendering this call, however unintentionally so, not only classist, but also indirectly racist.

(I also note in that essay that there is a plethora of ways in which living in a rural or less-vegan-friendly area can *help* rather than hinder you in contributing to the Animal Liberation Movement, such as by facilitating the creation or maintenance of a nonhuman animal sanctuary; and by enabling you to protest sites of violence such as slaughterhouses and nonhuman animal farms, which are not to be found in downtown Berkeley.)

c) A major animal rights conference has, for many years now, continued to invite a specific person to speak and promote his work. I am afraid to even type his name for fear of being sued, as many— possibly all— of his accusers have been. This man has been accused over and over again of sexual harassment, yet he has slapped at least several of his accusers with the aptly-named SLAPP suit.

Here's what Wikipedia has to say about SLAPP suits:

> *A* ***strategic lawsuit against public participation (SLAPP)*** *is a lawsuit that is intended to censor, intimidate and silence critics by burdening them with the cost of a legal defense until they abandon their criticism or opposition. Such lawsuits have been made illegal in many jurisdictions on the grounds that they impede freedom of speech.*
>
> *The typical SLAPP plaintiff does not normally expect to win the lawsuit. The plaintiff's goals are accomplished if the defendant succumbs to fear, intimidation, mounting legal costs or simple exhaustion and abandons the criticism.*[11]

Year after year, I am shocked, heartbroken and baffled to see this individual's name front and center on A.R. conference billings. This illustrates a disturbing lack of commitment among organizers within the Animal Liberation Movement towards the liberation of human women and is one of many reasons I personally abstain from attending certain conferences.

I eagerly await the moment when the #MeToo Movement— an anti-sexual-predation movement that began in October 2017, in the wake of revelations of myriad sexual abuses committed by film producer Harvey Weinstein— catches on in the animal liberation community. It is so desperately needed.

Clearly, there is work to be done in the realm of nonhuman animal advocacy with respect to displaying solidarity with humans. On the other side of the coin, many human advocacy groups regularly host parties, meetings, conferences and other events at which meat, dairy, sea creatures, and eggs are served and consumed without a moment's hesitation.

True solidarity across causes cannot be reduced to a singular event or campaign. Many nonhuman animal advocacy groups have, for instance, spent a single day assisting an organization that does not obviously promote nonhuman rights. These groups proceed to post images on social media and employ hashtags to perpetuate the myth that they are in fact uniting with the non-vegan-centric organization. These events as thus reduced to photo ops used as propaganda for the *vegan* organization while achieving little for whatever the "other" cause is.

Solidarity with "other" movements— that is to say, solidarity with other manifestations of the singular leftist movement for the liberation of all sentient beings— must be absolutely and unequivocally consistent and focused in nature in order to have any measurable value. Activists who traditionally focus on one cause within this movement for liberation must routinely demonstrate support for others by assisting at events, showing up for protests and rallies, participating in fundraisers, and so forth. A single afternoon spent working for another cause means precious little if you never return, and posting, for instance, a Black Lives Matter hashtag after months of remaining silent on the issue— particularly at the start of the movement, when protests in Baltimore were picking up steam in April 2015, and *any* organization that considered itself a "social justice organization" should have been publicly supporting them— smacks of opportunism.

There is reason to remain hopeful. Black Lives Matter, for instance, has made a tremendous declaration of solidarity with Palestinians by publicly supporting Boycott, Divestment and Sanctions (BDS).[12] In so doing, Black Lives Matter members made clear that their ultimate aim is not to achieve justice and prosperity "just for black folks" but to achieve these for *all* folks— including those overseas whom they have never met. While the unfortunate truth is that every U.S. American contributes financially to the illegal settlement of the West Bank by the current Israeli administration when they pay their taxes, supporting BDS illustrates that as much as it is within one's power to do so, one will abstain from financing oppression, no matter where it is happening, whom it is happening to, or whether the government perpetrating it is a U.S. ally or not.

Food Empowerment Project,[13] originally mentioned in this book's essay "Animal Agriculture: An Injustice to Humans and Nonhumans Alike," is another shining example of solidarity at work. Two programs of theirs that illustrate this beautifully are their sister website, VeganMexicanFood.Com, and their annual school supplies drive. Rather than telling Mexicans to abandon their culinary traditions and adopt vegan "white-people food" as their mealtime staples, the Food Empowerment Project regularly publicizes recipes that include traditional Mexican ingredients and techniques *that also just happen to be vegan.* This illustrates their simultaneous respect for nonhuman animals and Mexicans, without prioritizing one over the other. Their annual school supplies drive helps to supply myriad children of farmers with essentials for academic success, demonstrating that their commitment to food issues extends *beyond* nonhuman animal issues and *beyond* culinary cultures to include the very humans who produce much of our nation's food: farmers.

I am hard-pressed to think of another organization with "food" in its name that would collect school supplies for children. That is the extent to which Food Empowerment Project truly excels at solidarity. Theirs is not a "choose your pet issue and run with it" organization; it's a "here are a bunch of related issues; how can we begin to solve them all?" organization.

Over the past few years, I have had to walk away from not one but *two* food justice groups for showing a lack of solidarity with specific humans— whether by launching offensive campaigns, supporting other groups in spite of their offensive campaigns, or mistreating their own members and/or members of the public. I am also wholly unwilling to shell out for a ticket to animal rights conferences so long as they continue to welcome accused sex offenders and organizations that openly partake in the exploitation of women.

"In fighting against Man, we must not come to resemble him."

—Old Major, *Animal Farm* by George Orwell[14]

We have got to get this right. Time is running out. Humans, nonhuman animals, and our planet are suffering and dying, and we cannot help them if we are constantly offending, ignoring and alienating one another. It is imperative that food justice advocates embrace veganism, while vegans consider the plight of humans as well as nonhumans in creating what they eat (or wear, or watch…). By taking a consistent stance against all oppression, we can avoid perpetuating the very forms of oppression we seek to abolish.

Citations

1. Sanbonmatsu, John. *The Postmodern Prince: Critical Theory, Left Strategy, and the Making of a New Political Subject.* New York: Monthly Review Press, August 2003.

2. "Intersectionality." Wikipedia entry. Accessed June 18, 2018.

3. Sheth, Sonam. Skye Gould. "Five Charts Show How Much More Men Make than Women." *Business Insider*, March 8, 2017.

4. "Equal Pay for Black Women." Published by the National Women's Law Center. July 27, 2017.

5. "Equal Pay for Latinas." Published by the National Women's Law Center and the Labor Council for Latin American Advancement. October 2016.

6. "Equal Pay for Native Women." Published by the National Women's Law Center. September 21, 2017.

7. Feliz-Brueck, Julia. *Veganism in an Oppressive World.* Switzerland: Sanctuary Publishers, November 2017.

8. Hood, Micaela. "PETA Pokes Fun of Donald Trump with New 'Grab a Pussy!' Campaign." *New York Daily News,* October 13, 2016.

9. Leonard, Tom. "Not So Cuddly: What Stars Who Strip for Animal Rights Charity Need to Know about its Hate-Filled Home Counties Leader." *The Daily Mail*, November 20, 2015.

10. Hsiung, Wayne. "Should I Move…for the Animals? Lessons from Occupy Wall Street." *The Liberationist,* originally published August 11, 2015.

11. "Strategic lawsuit against public participation." Wikipedia entry. Accessed June 18, 2018.

12. Lewis, Renee. "African-American Rights Activists Endorse Boycott of Israel." *Al Jazeera*, August 19, 2015.

13. Food Empowerment Project Home Page.

14. Orwell, George. *Animal Farm.* England: Secker and Warburg, August 1945.

ABOUT THE CONTRIBUTORS

Helen Atthowe farms and conducts research on a 211-acre farm in Eastern Oregon. She also creates educational videos with her husband, which can be found on YouTube under the name AgrarianDreams. Helen has an M.S. in Horticulture from Rutgers University and worked at Rutgers and the University of Arkansas in Tree Fruit Integrated Pest Management and Orchard Management. From 1993-2010, Helen was a Horticulture Extension Agent, taught an organic Master Garden course, and owned/operated a thirty-acre certified organic vegetable/fruit farm in Montana. Helen wrote grants and conducted several on-farm research projects, including: ecological weed and insect management, organic reduced tillage systems for vegetable crops, and managing living mulches for soil and habitat building (results available at: http://articles.extension.org/pages/73949/organic-farm-system:-biodesign-farm).

From 2012-2015, Helen farmed with her husband at Woodleaf Farm in California and worked part-time as a research assistant for Oregon State University, studying several long-term, organic farms. Helen was a board member for the Organic Farming Research Foundation from 2000-2005. More about her work can be found at VeganicPermaculture.com.

Michelle Carrera is a Latinx vegan food justice activist. She is the founder of both Chilis on Wheels and its new Vegan Community Center in Puerto Rico. She is the co-founder of Latinos for Animal Protection and organized the Vegan Latinos of NYC Meetup from 2015-2017. She is an Unschooling mother, translator, and writer. Her passions include minimalism, modern and historic nomadic tendencies, and community building.

Starr Carrington is a queer Black vegan from Northern Virginia. Starr is a facilitator, author, Black vegan activist and food justice researcher who approaches her activism through the lenses of Black feminism and food justice. She is currently pursuing a Bachelor's degree in Psychology with a minor in African and African-American studies at George Mason University, where she has participated in an independent study named "Black Woman's Health: Mind, Body and Soul."

Through her social handle, BlackFeministVegan, Starr advocates for food justice, provides educational resources, and shares transitional tips specifically for Black and brown people. Her work aims to address missing links to social revolution within the mainstream vegan movement. She is the founder of a nonprofit organization called Fuel the People, which works to serve, empower, and provide vegan awareness for the Black community through free food distribution, food justice education and community outreach projects.

Julia Feliz Brueck is an AfroLatinx born and raised in Puerto Rico. She is the founder of Sanctuary Publishers, a vegan book publisher with the aim of supporting all marginalized communities through content and sales. Julia is also the founder of VeganismOfColor.com, a hub by vegans of color for people of color in an effort to form bridges between social justice movements through consistent anti-oppression– inclusive of both nonhumans and humans. Julia also holds undergraduate and graduate degrees in the biological sciences, including conservation ecology, and she is an editor, as well as a published author and art illustrator. Her most recent published books include ***Veganism in an Oppressive World: A Vegans-of-Color Community Project*** and the ***Baby and Toddler Vegan Feeding Guide***. You can follow Julia's publishing work on SanctuaryPublishers.com and JuliaFeliz.com.

Dawn Moncrief is the founding director of A Well-Fed World, an international vegan hunger relief and animal protection organization. A Well-Fed World's dual mission uniquely assists both humans *and* nonhumans in dire need. Their research and advocacy create structural change by advancing the global food security benefits of plant-based foods and farming. Their grant-making and movement-building programs provide immediate material and financial assistance that empowers grassroots food justice and farmed animal rescue groups. A Well-Fed World's organizational partners include the International Fund for Africa, Grow Where You Are, and MaituFoods. In addition to presenting research in the U.S., U.K., Europe, and Africa, Dawn has chapters in a variety of anthologies, the most relevant here is her chapter, "Hunger, Meat, and the Banality of Evil" in ***Circles of Compassion: Essays Connecting Issues of Justice.***

Saryta Rodríguez is an author, editor, and social justice advocate. Their first book, ***Until Every Animal is Free***, was published in October 2015 by Vegan Publishers. Saryta also contributed an essay, "Move to Berkeley! and Other Follies," as well as part of the Introduction (regarding the distinction between *intersectionality* and *diversity*) to ***Veganism in an Oppressive World: A Vegans-of-Color Community Project*** (published in November 2017 by

Sanctuary Publishers). Their past writings have focused on food justice, veganism, race, and gentrification, with articles appearing on such notable social justice websites as *Free From Harm*, *Causa Justa/Just Cause*, and *Reasonable Vegan*. Saryta currently edits for Sanctuary Publishers, while also accepting unrepresented clients. Originally from Bay Shore, New York, they currently reside in Harlem. Essays by and interviews with Saryta can be found at SarytaRodriguez.com.

Lilia Trenkova was born and raised in Bulgaria during the final years of communism, before emigrating to the U.S. in 2000. They reside in Brooklyn with their human partner, Raffi, and adopted nonhuman, Pumpkin. Lili works as an architectural/environmental designer, scenic artist and fabricator, and organizes with Collectively Free, a pro-intersectional animal rights community they and Raffi co-founded in 2014.

ACKNOWLEDGMENTS

This book would not have been possible without the help, support, and contributions of myriad individuals. First and foremost, I would like to thank all of my fellow contributors— Dawn Moncrief, Lilia Trenkova, Starr Carrington, Michelle Carrera, and Helen Atthowe— for sharing their insights and perspectives, as well as for all of the work they do to contribute to food justice in their communities.

I am also deeply grateful to Gustavo Oliviera for his illuminating interview, as well as for suggesting sources for background study regarding land rights movements. His experience participating in a variety of food justice and land rights struggles was invaluable to me and is an inspiration to us all.

My sincerest thanks to my publisher, Julia Feliz Brueck, for all of the time and effort she put into editing this book and ushering it through the production process.

Finally, I would like to thank everyone who takes the time and expends the effort to contribute to food justice, in whatever form that takes. Whether you have gone vegan; engage in food distribution to those in need; support legislation to protect those working in the food industry; read labels and do research on the food items you eat— and the companies that produce them— to ensure they are ethically sourced; donate money or supplies to organizations such as the Food Empowerment Project, Grow Where You Are, Chilis on Wheels, or A Well-Fed World; or all of the above, every little bit helps. The ways you can contribute are numerous, and I thank you now both for what you are currently doing and for what I am sure you will commit to in the future as your knowledge of and passion about this important issue develops.